Before the Resurrection

Before the Resurrection

Transitions and Endings in Quaker
Meetings and Churches

Emily Provance

RESOURCE *Publications* · Eugene, Oregon

BEFORE THE RESURRECTION
Transitions and Endings in Quaker Meetings and Churches

Copyright © 2025 Emily Provance. All rights reserved. Except for brief quotations in critical publications or reviews, no part of this book may be reproduced in any manner without prior written permission from the publisher. Write: Permissions, Wipf and Stock Publishers, 199 W. 8th Ave., Suite 3, Eugene, OR 97401.

Resource Publications
An Imprint of Wipf and Stock Publishers
199 W. 8th Ave., Suite 3
Eugene, OR 97401

www.wipfandstock.com

PAPERBACK ISBN: 979-8-3852-2868-3
HARDCOVER ISBN: 979-8-3852-2869-0
EBOOK ISBN: 979-8-3852-2870-6

VERSION NUMBER 03/19/25

Scriptures taken from the Holy Bible, New International Version®, NIV®. Copyright © 1973, 1978, 1984, 2011 by Biblica, Inc.™ Used by permission of Zondervan. All rights reserved worldwide. www.zondervan.com The "NIV" and "New International Version" are trademarks registered in the United States Patent and Trademark Office by Biblica, Inc.™

Contents

Acknowledgments and Methodology | vii
Introduction | ix

Corporate Discernment | 1
The Life Cycle of Meetings | 5
Structural Mismatches: When the Institution Does
    Not Support the Community | 10
Naming Our Condition | 13
Institutional Adaptations | 16
Why Adapting Is Hard | 19
The Process of Adapting | 24
For Clerks of Local Meetings | 32
For Pastors | 37
For Record Keepers | 40
For Trustees | 42
For Regional or Yearly Meeting Clerks or Staff | 45
Ghost Meetings | 50
For Traveling Ministers | 55
Conflict | 58
Changing the Committee Structure | 62
Staff Transitions | 68
Hybrid and Online Meetings | 71
Combining or Merging Meetings | 73

Restructuring the Local Meeting | 81
Taking a Meeting "Under Our Care" | 86
Property | 92
Laying Down a Meeting | 96
On Archives | 103
Pastoral Care in Transitions and Endings | 104
Transitions and Endings for Regional Meetings | 107
Transitions and Endings for Yearly Meetings | 114
What Resurrection Might Look Like | 125
A Conversation Guide for Friends Using Readings from the Bible | 129
A Conversation Guide for Friends Using Readings
   from Early Quakerism | 134

Bibliography | 137

Acknowledgments and Methodology

My work on the life cycle of meetings began with a post on social media. "Who do I know who is concerned about endings for Quaker meetings?" I got dozens of replies. A group of Friends came together for regular conversations and research. That group included Michael Booth, Dorothy Grannell, Susan Hoskins, Callie Janoff, Sandy Kewman, Hannah Mullikin Lutz, Robin Mohr, Helen Mullin, Anne Pomeroy, Kathy Slattery, and Nia Thomas.

Others joined one-time conversations or carried out practical tasks or wrote articles for publications. These included Carl Abbott, Margery Post Abbott, Don Badgley, Astuti Bijlefeld, Chris Cradler, Larry Ferguson, the Friends General Conference New Meetings Project, Gil George, Pip Harris, Nikki Holland, Janet Hough, Esmé Ingledew, J.P. Lund, Philip Maurer, John Moru, Nicolas Otieno, Colin Saxton, West Newton Friends Meeting, and Kathleen Wooten.

More than eighty Friends attended a one-time online consultation in November of 2022 about the life cycle of meetings. In April 2023, 272 individuals from 148 local meetings participated in a series of twenty online consultations exploring transitions and endings.

Three of my most important ecumenical contacts have been Marilyn Fiddmont, David Shoen, and the Good Friday Collaborative. I learned from dozens of other books and articles produced by clergy and lay people of various traditions. Many of those titles are listed in the "additional resources" section at the end of this book.

Financial support for related publications came from the Mosher Fund of New England Yearly Meeting and from an anonymous private donor. The Friends World Committee for Consultation Section of the Americas

Acknowledgments and Methodology

provided significant logistical help. I also learned from the data gathered in FWCC's 2022 census of Quaker meetings in the United States.

My own ministry is supported by dozens of donors. Their generosity releases me to take on projects with no obvious avenue of financial support. I'm also an associate of Good News Associates, a Christian nonprofit ministry organization supporting individuals who are called to non-institutional ministries. According to Friends' tradition, my ministry is affirmed by, and I am accountable to, Fifteenth Street Meeting in New York City. For this project, I also received significant grant support from the Louisville Institute.

Many of the individuals and groups listed above have more direct experience with transitions and endings for faith communities than I do. It has been my task to gather their collective wisdom and to discern a sort of "sense of the meeting." This is challenging when the group contributing is not gathered in a single conversation. I am sure I have discerned imperfectly, but I have tried my best.

The author wishes to acknowledge grant support from the Louisville Institute.

Introduction

WHEN A PERSON DIES, the last sense to disappear is hearing. This is why, when a loved one is dying, we're encouraged to speak to them, even if their eyes are closed and they can't squeeze our hands. A hospital chaplain reminded me of this when I interviewed her for this book. "You keep emphasizing the Quaker practice of deep listening," she said. "Did you know that people can hear even at the very end of life?" This book assumes that Friends' meetings and churches can, too—that a group of Friends assembled can always hear from God, even if the faith community is dying.

All living things age and die, and a Quaker meeting is a living thing. Corporate worship teaches me so. The Holy Spirit animates a meeting with a Life force that is *more* than the essences of the people within it. I've been with meetings and churches around the world, and I know that they—like people—are precious and unique, set apart for some particular purpose. They're born with a spark of life, and they grow, and they die. They inherit teachings, culture, procedures, and assumptions from meetings that came before them. They keep some of these; they reject some of these. They go through periods of thriving and struggling, of resting and acting, of hope and of grief. They engage with wider communities, giving and receiving both material and immaterial things. And when they die, they leave legacies.

This is a book about the aging and death of beloved spiritual communities. You'll find resources about laying down a Quaker meeting, but not only that. Just like people, a meeting has to adjust as it ages. It needs to change its habits to better reflect its life stage. If it does, it can thrive in new ways in its old age. So you'll find guidance here, too, on some steps a meeting might take during the aging process before its end.

Introduction

The biggest difference between an aging human and an aging meeting is that we *know* a human will age and die. We see models of this from our earliest consciousness. But in the case of a Quaker meeting or other spiritual community, we convince ourselves that it's possible for the institution to live forever. We often want to believe this, partly because we love our meeting and partly because the culture around us says "more is better" and "endings are failures." But neither of those things is universally true.

Quakers are a resurrection people, beginning with the story of Jesus. We demonstrate our faith in resurrection every time we enter corporate discernment, fully expecting the inbreaking of Light. Redemption is always possible, even when our circumstances have pushed us to the brink of despair.

But resurrection is not the same as resuscitation. Early Friends emphasized spiritual transformation, not spiritual restoration. When have we ever said that God's will is to maintain the status quo? In research and interviews and direct experience, I've come to see that when we stop fighting for resuscitation—when we lay down a meeting or make changes to reflect its actual condition—we release spiritual energy that can then be repurposed. As a United Church of Christ minister once said to me, "What might God do that won't happen here?"

From our beginnings, Friends have said that human beings do not make things true. God makes them true, and we write them down. This is why early Friends recorded ministers but did not ordain them. No earthly ceremony, they said, could make a person a minister. Only God could do that. Our job was noticing and then acting accordingly. The same was true of other sacraments, including baptism, communion, and marriage. Early Friends did not eliminate these but believed that God would enact them spiritually and that we Friends would then recognize them.

I believe it's the same when we make changes in our meetings. To lay down a meeting does not cause a meeting to die. It is a faithful recognition that the meeting has come to the end of its life. Similarly, to restructure a meeting or merge it or lay down some committees does not cause a meeting to age. It is a faithful recognition that the meeting is aging. We are responding to a pre-existing spiritual truth.

Sometimes Friends wonder if transitions or endings in a Quaker meeting somehow dishonor or spoil what came before. They say, "Don't we have a responsibility to our ancestors to keep it going?" Or, "I've been worshiping here for thirty-five years. I was married in this meeting. It can't be laid down." These are normal feelings. If we love our meeting, any change

Introduction

or ending will cause us to grieve. But the end of a thing does not make its history less precious. God has done incredible things here! Let's honor and celebrate that—and make space, as well, for what God will do next.

It might help to know that we're not alone. In the United States, most mainline Christian denominations have lost a third or more of their members in the last twenty-five years.[1] As much as 24% of Quaker meetings in the United States may have been laid down or disaffiliated between 2010 and 2020.[2] We're in the midst of a massive societal shift, in which church attendance and membership are dropping swiftly (except in some evangelical traditions). This is nobody's fault. It simply is. It also makes me wonder, again, what new thing God might be planning for Friends. If the future of Quakerism won't be the traditional meeting structure, what might it be? "See, I am doing a new thing! Now it springs up; do you not perceive it?" (Isaiah 43:19)

No, we often do not perceive it. No matter how well I understand the statistics, my own precious meeting is not a number on paper. It is my home. It is the place where I have met God and been transformed. No matter how much I believe in resurrection, no matter how fully I understand the big picture, what happens to my own spiritual community will always feel deeply personal.

When I talk about transitions and endings for Quaker meetings, Friends' reactions vary considerably. Some express an immediate sense of relief. They have known that their meeting is aging or dying. They're grateful for support in saying this out loud. Others react with denial or anger. Any of these responses is normal and a good enough place to start.

It's important to know that nothing in this book is intended to encourage any meeting to take any specific action. In fact, it's vital that a meeting discerns its own future, and this book is intended to support Friends in doing that. The discernment process can be confusing—is the meeting dying, or is it changing? And if changing, in what way? It's not always easy to tell, and again, this book can help by explaining some common patterns. But no checklist can tell Friends the faithful next steps for their meeting. Only corporate discernment can do that.

If you're wondering whether your meeting is near its end, this book is for you.

1. Woolf, "Denominations Are Dying."
2. Friends World Committee of Consultation Section of the Americas, "FWCC Census of Friends Shows Declines, But More Research Is Needed."

Introduction

If you don't believe your meeting is nearing its end, but you're sensing that some kind of changes are needed, this book is also for you. It's not all or nothing. Long before we're ready for the laying down process, there are steps we can take to help an aging meeting thrive.

If you're a Friend who works with meetings other than your own—as a regional clerk, a yearly meeting staff member, a traveling minister, or something else—this book is definitely for you. It will offer some perspective, gathered from interviews and conversations and texts, to frame some of what you're sensing about the condition of meetings. It will also offer suggestions about how you may respond.

No matter where you're standing, remember you're not alone. Quaker meetings exist in a web of connections. We can talk with other local meetings. We can ask for conversations to convene at retreat centers. We can seek the advice of Friends serving in parallel positions (treasurers with other treasurers, clerks with other clerks). We can even reach out to ecumenical and interfaith networks in our towns or counties. Relationship is nearly always available. No group needs to find its way in isolation.

Corporate Discernment

THE HEART OF THIS book is corporate discernment, so I'll start by explaining what that means. Friends believe in a balance between two principles: the individual's direct connection to God and the essential practice of discernment in community. Both of these ideas are extraordinarily powerful. Friends believe that God speaks directly to every individual. We can choose to listen or not. In the time and place of early Quakerism, this was a radical and counter-cultural idea. The dominant faith traditions of society said that priests interpreted the Bible and God's will. Today, many people believe in direct connection to the divine without intermediary. But the concept of continuing revelation—God actively speaking—is still radical. Friends listen not to our own best selves but to something beyond our full understanding, and we seek to be faithful to what we hear.

The discipline of listening is a lifelong practice. It is hard, we have learned over many generations, to discern the difference between God's voice and the noise of other internal and external forces. This is why we practice corporate discernment. A Friend who is making an important decision may ask for other Friends to gather around her, praying and posing queries to evoke reflection. Sometimes we call this a clearness committee. In helps the individual Friend in question to hear from God a little more clearly.

And when the community faces a collective decision, we gather in worship for a meeting for business. Through speaking, silence, prayer, and sometimes Scripture study or other readings, we discover the *sense of the meeting*.

Corporate discernment differs from consensus. We are not seeking compromise. It is more than that; we are seeking the will of God. This is both profound and quite ordinary. When we discern, we're not seeking the will of God for all people in all circumstances. That's much too big. Instead, we're seeking the will of God for us, this group gathered here, at this time and in this place. You might say we're seeking the next faithful step. Caroline Fox said, "Live up to the light thou hast, and more will be granted thee." God usually offers guidance one step at a time.

To practice corporate discernment is to trust each other. Early Friends quickly discovered that when we listen to God independently, we all tend to get somewhat different results. As a friend of mine says, "Sometimes the water tastes of the pipes." Our previous experiences, our egos, our cultures, our desires, our relationships, even whether we're hungry that day can influence what we think we hear. For this reason, Friends believe that to listen alone is to listen incompletely. The truth discovered by the group as a whole will be closer to the truth God is giving us.

When I enter corporate discernment, I have some responsibilities to the community. Each Friend's responsibilities are the same.

First is my responsibility to *speak*. I need not speak to every question posed in the meeting—in fact, if I did, that would probably be an indication that I was speaking too often. But when my perception of God's will or the truth of the situation differs from that of the Friends who have already spoken, it's my responsibility to share what I see. If I stay silent out of shyness or embarrassment or because I am tired and want the meeting to end, I am not fulfilling my responsibility to the community.

Second is my responsibility to *release*. Once I have spoken, what I've said no longer belongs to me. It is as though we are working together to assemble a jigsaw puzzle. My spoken contribution is my puzzle piece. I lay it down in front of the community and step away. I don't insist upon where it should go in the puzzle or threaten to run away with it if I don't like the bigger picture.

Third is my responsibility to *discern*. As each voice is heard, I pay attention to my spiritual response, my emotions, my intellect, and my physical body, all of which might offer me cues about the truth of the contributions. I will probably start to see a bigger picture, a *sense of the meeting* that is the truth revealed by the whole community.

Fourth is my responsibility to *affirm*. At some point, someone in the room (probably the clerk, but not always) will put into words what she thinks the sense of the meeting might be. It's not relevant whether the sense of the meeting does or does not agree with my individual perception. What's relevant is whether the articulated statement is an accurate reflection of the bigger picture, the truth as revealed by the whole community. If it is, I can affirm it—because I trust the community's discernment over my own.

Last is my responsibility to *unify*. After the meeting is over, I carry out the sense of the meeting. What the group has discerned is what we will do. It can be tempting, at times, to feel disgruntled or complain or resist next steps, especially if the sense of the meeting goes against my best individual judgment, but to do so undermines the discipline of corporate discernment and erodes the mutual trust in my community.

These practices can be difficult even in the best of times, perhaps especially with a community I know well and love. The decisions we make together are important to me. Also, as is often said, no one can annoy us quite as much as the people we love most dearly. But corporate discernment might feel even harder when we're working toward transitions or endings for our Quaker meeting. These sorts of matters carry tremendous emotional, practical, and spiritual weight.

Corporate discernment is at the heart of Quaker practice, and for this reason it's essential that the meeting discerns its own future. It's also essential for another reason, which is this: *the process of discernment is, itself, what prepares us to accept the results of that discernment.* To practice corporate discernment is to embark on a collective journey. We begin with a question, perhaps more than one. We listen deeply to God and to each other. We express emotion. We consider logistics. We witness the mutual commitment of the people around us. We have a spiritual experience that's both communal and internal, and that experience softens our hearts, opens our minds, and teaches us what God would have us do in this moment.

Anyone who's ever missed a significant business meeting will understand this concept instinctively. When I hear the results of discernment after the fact, the community's decision may seem strange, even counterintuitive. It may be hard to accept. It's possible, of course, that had I been present, I would have brought some piece of truth the community was missing, and the end result would have been different. But even if it would not have been, I have missed the process that would have prepared me to understand and accept the sense of the meeting. I can trust my community regardless and unify with their discernment, but that might feel hard, especially if I don't like the decision.

A meeting discerns its own future, but who is "the meeting?" When we're considering significant transitions or endings—such as merging with another meeting, or restructuring as a worship group, or laying the meeting down, or selling our property—it probably isn't just the people who show up for worship. It might include members who have moved away. It might include the children or grandchildren of Friends in the meeting who grew up attending our Sunday school. It might include Friends in the region who have frequently visited us. And especially if we're dealing with matters related to property, it might include the people in the neighborhood—because our decisions will affect them, too.

During discernment about transitions and endings, it's important to cast the net wide and to do so early on. That's partly for spiritual reasons, so that the whole meeting can discern the meeting's future. But it's also for practical reasons. If less active or far away Friends aren't aware of the discernment process and at least given an option to participate, they may appear at the last minute unprepared to accept the results of the discernment—and that can throw a wrench in the works.

Part of what you'll find in this book is strategies for including various groups in your discernment process in ways that are supportive, open-hearted, and also practical. You'll also find, in the various chapters, a number of different types of transitions or endings that a Quaker meeting might consider. We don't often experience a leading to do something we've never heard of. It can happen—God is great—but it's easier to envision way forward if we have first seen examples.

The most important thing is trust: trust in God, trust in community, and trust in ourselves. We can always expect to be guided if we listen.

The Life Cycle of Meetings

Humans start life as a bundle of possibilities. Part of who we'll become is predetermined, decreed by genetics and environment and culture. But mostly the future is gloriously unknown. We grow, and as we do, we develop strengths and skills and habits. Through trial and error, we find our particular way of approaching the world. We form relationships. Some of these are determined by proximity. Others we choose according to preference. We may develop a sense of purpose that guides us. The experiences we have during growth and adolescence will shape our personalities and many of our major life decisions.

Later, as we mature, we settle into a pattern of living. We become more predictable. There are still possibilities—new paths that might be taken—but there are probably things we're sure we'll never do. We become highly competent in particular areas. We take fewer risks than we did in our youth. If we reproduce, this is also the stage of life in which we're parenting.

By age sixty, we enter what some call the last third of life. We've gathered a lot of wisdom and perspective. We have much to offer in terms of skills and guidance for others, but we are probably slow to try radically new things. Some of us begin to resist change. We have less energy and, of necessity, we become more selective about what we'll do. In our final years, we may need help with the basic functions of living. Eventually, we die.

Many of us live in cultures that lionize youth. I've been grateful for recent movements among Friends to celebrate and honor the last third of life, in which there is still so much to do and be. God can speak through anyone, regardless of age, and much is lost when our society scorns or patronizes its oldest living generations.

Before the Resurrection

The life cycle description above is a generalization, of course. No real human existence aligns exactly with a theoretical process. We have periods of growth and periods of stasis throughout our life cycles at unpredictable times. Sudden crises can shift our habits radically. Personalities can be reformed. Some fifteen-year-olds are wise and cautious and settled, and some sixty-five-year-olds thrive on risk. But the general pattern of a human life is sufficiently accurate to be a useful idea.

Life stages are so recognizable and so important to humans that we have rituals to mark transitions between them. In many Muslim cultures, a father whispers a call to prayer in a child's ear just after birth. Many Jewish children celebrate a bar mitzvah or bat mitzvah to mark the arrival into adulthood. Nearly every culture has rituals around marriage, which historically has been the start of a new family. We celebrate puberty, pregnancy, retirement, coming of age, graduations, and even death.

To mark a transition is to honor change. We've been one sort of person; we will now be another. The ritual allows us to reset expectations. After graduation, we don't go back to high school. After retirement, day-to-day life will be different. Even if we're not ready for the change (and we often don't feel ready), we acknowledge that it's happening.

Faith communities also have a life cycle, but that can be much harder to see. Most of us know many more humans than we do faith communities. We have all known a person who has died. Many of us have never seen the end of a Quaker meeting. Because we haven't had models of this other kind of life cycle, and because we don't talk about it very often, we can easily believe that our meeting needn't age or die. We may not realize—either because we weren't present or because we don't mark the transitions as we do for humans—that our meeting has already passed through a number of life stages. The aging process is happening whether we recognize it or not.

Take a look at the diagramed model of the life cycle of a Quaker meeting. It will be easy to find reasons to say, "But this is not the experience of my faith community." Just like humans, no individual meeting proceeds through these stages predictably. Sometimes we have a crisis and suddenly leap forward a stage. Sometimes we go back a stage. We have periods of growth and periods of stasis throughout the life cycle at unpredictable times. Nevertheless, the general pattern is sufficiently accurate to be a useful idea.

The Life Cycle of Meetings

Before we delve into the individual life stages, I invite you to notice two things about this image. First: the stages overlap. This is true for humans, as well. We do not transform from adolescence to adulthood at the precise moment of a coming-of-age ritual. The ritual makes obvious a transition that's actually quite gradual. Absent a ritual, it's hard to notice the transition, which is a theme that will come up a lot in this book. And second: the final circle, death, is higher than the circle representing birth. When a Quaker meeting dies, everything does not return to exactly like it was. The meeting's life has made a difference. It leaves behind something that did not exist before.

Which of the descriptions below feels like your meeting or a meeting you know? The answer might be "more than one," which is fine. This work is messy, and the stages overlap. You also might answer one way now and later change your mind. This is simply a place to start.

Birth: We feel energized, and the future is full of possibilities. We've been led to start this meeting in this time and this place. We know who we are, and we know why we exist. . .but there are so many questions about what will happen next!

Infancy: Every week is a new discovery. It's pretty easy to try new things because we don't really have any habits. If something doesn't work, we just do it differently next time. Our group is still pretty small. The meeting might not even be a legally independent entity.

Becoming: The meeting probably has its own building and legal status. We're getting a system going. We mostly know how things get done, but our ways of working together are still developing. We still make a lot of mistakes, and we have a learning-new-things, try-again mindset. There are newcomers and new ministries and participants from all stages of life, and the meeting feels like an exciting place to be.

Maturity: Deeply committed Friends are doing vital work. The neighborhood community around us knows who we are. We're confident in our identity as a meeting, and we feel sure that we have a future. Our financial situation is pretty solid. The average age of Friends attending has gone up, but only a little.

Stability: We're very good at maintaining the status quo. The number of families in the meeting is declining, but we might have an increasing number of older adults. We don't usually try new or risky things. We don't remember (or no longer feel) the excitement of the meeting when it was new.

Aging: Fewer people are attending regularly, which makes it hard to keep ministries and programming going. Our finances are shrinking. We feel nostalgic. We might have more conflict than we used to.

Infirmity: Friends are tired. They've started resigning from their committee assignments and ministry roles, often without much advanced notice. Positions go unfilled. Finances are shaky. Most of us are elderly. We are not able to do meaningful ministry in our neighborhood community.

Death: We might have worship, but not much else. We can't manage upkeep for property, nurture of ministries, or religious education. It's hard to hold meetings for business. If our meeting will be revived, we think it will happen because new people appeared. We ourselves cannot reenergize it.

Do you have an initial reaction to these descriptions? Where would you place your own Quaker meeting? How does the act of naming that feel?

It's important, yet again, to go back to recognizing the messages of our wider society, the insistence that more is better and that youth has virtue while aging does not. We know this isn't true, and yet some of us feel an instinctive desire for our meetings to be vigorous, or a sense that aging is equivalent to failure. But this does not reflect the nature of God. Just as God can speak through anyone, God can do amazing things through any meeting. We can be faithful in every stage. But an "aging" meeting and a "becoming" meeting need different things in order to thrive, and that's what most of this book is about: recognizing where we are and adjusting.

Regarding the very end of the life cycle, you'll notice that a meeting in the death stage does not, in fact, automatically end. If no one takes initiative to lay down the meeting, it might continue in this stage for many years. Eventually, the Friends in the meeting will, themselves, die or move away, and the meeting will become a "ghost meeting," existing in a technical sense but not capable of discerning its own future. When this happens, the faith community doesn't have a chance to think consciously about establishing a legacy, which is a loss. I'll say more about this later, when speaking specifically about the process of laying down a meeting.

We've now reached the point in the conversation when many Friends say, "I think my meeting's in the second half of the life cycle, but...can't we grow and thrive again?"

The answer is yes, it is usually possible, except if the meeting has reached the very end of its life cycle. (There's a reason the description of the death stage says, "we ourselves can't reenergize the meeting." We literally can't. We lack the energy, the resources, and/or the ability.)

I often work with Quaker meetings that are trying to grow. When I first started ministry related to outreach and intergenerational inclusion, I'd leap immediately to talking about how it can be done—which I won't be detailing here, because that would be a whole different book. But in time, I learned that *how it can be done* is the wrong starting point, because many communities of Friends aren't actually led to grow. They simply believe that they *should* want to grow, partly because our society constantly sends us messages that more is better.

The meeting that is truly led to grow will also be a meeting that is led to change. Growth does not exist without change. New people bring new energy, new ideas, new practices, new noise, new wall decorations, new ministries, new life. And newness—though glorious—is a lot of work and inevitably disrupts our comfort and our routines. If a community is not genuinely open to change, it will resist change, which makes it very hard to welcome newcomers.

If God is not calling your community to grow, that's okay. It's okay to be who you are. It is okay to be a meeting in the stability or aging phase. It is okay to stay in those phases, if God is not calling you to grow. God can do powerful work through any meeting in any life stage.

Also, though this may feel counterintuitive, working on growth and working on aging are not necessarily in conflict. An aging meeting can adjust its structures appropriately while simultaneously practicing outreach and intergenerational inclusion. In fact, a meeting's adjustments for aging may release energy that can be used for growth. That's part of what I mean when I talk about resurrection.

Structural Mismatches
When the Institution Does Not Support the Community

WHEN WE TALK ABOUT a Quaker meeting, we need to distinguish between the institution and the community. When I reference the institution, I'm thinking of the legal status of the meeting, the procedural set-up (committee structures, written handbooks, budgets), and the official relationships with other groups of Friends (such as affiliations with yearly meetings or other organizations). The institution might also include the administration of community ministries, such as soup kitchens or tutoring programs.

The meeting institution is not the same as the meeting community, which is the group of people that has come together. I frame the community through the lens of covenant, which I've heard defined as "we give ourselves to God, and God in turn gives us to a group of people." We are united as a community by the divine and by our collective commitment to faithfulness.

When we talk about "the meeting" as a shorthand, it's not always clear if we're referring to the group of people (the community) or the structural entity (the institution). We confuse these in our own minds sometimes. When we do so, we risk over-valuing the institution, which exists only for the purpose of supporting the community.

Let's put it another way. The faith community exists to be faithful. There are many ways to be faithful. For Quakers, collective faithfulness starts with deep listening to the Holy Spirit in the context of corporate discernment. Everything else we do is either preparation for this listening or a result of this listening. The outwardly visible activities of a meeting—community ministries, care for one another, religious education, witness and activism—are fruits of corporate discernment. Even Friends' testimonies have arisen from generations of corporate discernment, in keeping with the seventh chapter of Matthew's gospel: "ye shall know them by their fruits." In addition to this, many Friends experience individual leadings, from calls to ministry to gentle daily spiritual nudges. Our regular practice of deep listening in worship (regardless of whether our worship is programmed or unprogrammed) prepares us to hear and act on God's promptings.

We create Quaker institutions to support the community. If the community needs to worship each Sunday, it's helpful to have a building in which to do it, and that building needs care, so we form a building and grounds committee. If the community comes together in corporate discernment, it's helpful to have a designated person to create the agenda and conduct the meeting, so we nominate a clerk. If the community is called to open a used clothing shop for struggling neighbors, we will need flyers to advertise this and someone to answer the phone, so we buy a copier and hire an office administrator. And so forth.

The sole purpose of the Quaker institution is to support the community's faithfulness—but institutions tend to take on a life of their own. We hire an office administrator to support the used clothing shop. But if the demographics of the neighborhood change ten years later and the clothing shop is no longer needed, we find it hard to close it and fire the administrator. It seems so much easier to continue the status quo than to ask the big question: should we end this ministry? Asking causes conflict and difficult feelings.

Another example: we purchase a building in which to worship. Forty years later, our worship community is much smaller, and most of us live thirty miles to the east. We no longer need a large building in this neighborhood, but we find it hard to move. Our children's marriages took place in this building. The color of the walls is familiar and comforting. We like hosting the annual neighborhood Easter egg hunt. And so we continue caring for, and paying for, the building until *we* are serving *it* instead of *it* serving *us*.

This is what it looks like when there's a mismatch between our institutional structures and God's current calling for the community. We find ourselves in a situation in which the community is serving the institution, and not vice versa. More work goes into maintaining the committees, the property, the budget, the procedural requirements than goes into listening deeply to God. This is backwards. But it's remarkably easy to fall into.

For one thing, changes in the community happen gradually. As you read in an earlier section, the transitions from one life stage to the next are slow. The stages overlap. Sometimes we don't proceed neatly from one to the next but seem to bounce back and forth. We experience surges of activity and times of stasis. This makes us think, "Well, the building's too big for us now, but surely more people will come again." Or, "Well, the clothing shop isn't used much now, but surely it will be needed again." There is not a moment when the institutional structure is right-sized and then a moment when it's not. So it's easier, and it can seem quite reasonable, to simply let the institution perpetuate itself. Change takes a lot of energy—far more, in the short term, than just letting things continue—and on top of that, a mismatched institution chronically drains the energy of the community. So we're already tired. It can take a lot to initiate change in those circumstances.

Naming Our Condition

"Our institution isn't serving our community." That might not be exactly how we phrase it, but there's power in naming our condition out loud, and somebody has to be the first to do it.

How do we know if we have a structural mismatch? The signs will be different for different people. Some Friends rely mostly on spiritual knowing. They will have a sense of inherent off-kilter-ness. They know that something is wrong in the spiritual condition of the meeting. And they will be correct. A structural mismatch, though it sounds logistical, is a spiritual problem. The disproportionate time and energy we spend serving our own institution prevents us from living the fulness of the gospel.

Other Friends are most sensitive to people's emotional and physical conditions. They will see that members of the faith community seem tired, overwhelmed, angry, or numb. They will also be correct. A structural mismatch leads to exhaustion because of the energy needed to keep the institution going. And it produces conflict because different people see the problem differently (and some don't perceive it consciously at all). Many individuals may feel as though they are taking on a disproportionate share of the work. In some cases, this is true, but there is also probably too much work in total for the number of available individuals, so no matter how it's divided, it will feel unreasonable.

And other Friends learn the most from observable data and behaviors. For them, I offer the following assessment queries. The queries should not be used to dictate action, because of course it is corporate discernment by which we find our call to action, but the queries may help in assessing whether the meeting has a problem.

Before the Resurrection

Are fewer Friends at worship each week now as compared to five or ten years ago? The important indicator is not the size of the meeting. Some small meetings have rightly matched structures and are thriving. What's important is the change in size. If we have many fewer Friends in worship now than we did five or ten years ago, and if we haven't made significant changes in our structure, we likely have a mismatch.

Are we able to care for one another? No meeting can be all things to all of its members. A Friend in a serious or long-term crisis needs much more help than a meeting can give. But a meeting should be able to make a hospital visit, deliver meals to a Friend for a week or two, provide a prayer partner, or occasionally help with rent when someone has a shortfall. If we can't, we should ask ourselves where our energy and money are going and whether this feels rightly led.

Have we been covering our routine expenses using our savings? Or—do we have an oppressive amount of debt? Many Quaker meetings have occasional deficit years, so if our deficit years are truly "occasional," this might not be a cause for worry. But we might ask what would happen if the meeting's next five years are financially identical to the five most recent. If five or ten years of an ongoing pattern will lead our meeting to financial disaster, and if we have no particular reason to expect that we're about to discover buried treasure in the meetinghouse garden, then it's probably time to make some changes.

How is religious education going? It's not only newcomers who require discipleship. All of us need ongoing spiritual formation and reminders of basic Quaker practices. This might happen through study groups, Sunday school, worship sharing sessions, or watching videos together, but if the meeting has no religious education at all, it's a sign that time and energy are being pulled away from the community's theoretically spiritual focus.

Is it hard to figure out who's going to do the work? Having many empty committee slots is a sign of a meeting with an out-sized structure. The same is true if the meeting is relying on employees who are chronically underpaid. These are signs that the meeting might be called to do less in its new life stage.

Do we have thriving neighborhood and/or world ministries? Mutual care and spiritual formation of members is hugely important, but if the meeting is entirely focused inward, it's no longer fulling the essential roles of a meeting. A robust faith community will have some form of outward-facing ministry or ministries, although the substance of such ministries can vary widely. If the meeting can no longer respond to such calls, it is probably in one of the later stages of the life cycle.

Is the average age of attenders steadily increasing? We all get older every year. But if the average age of Friends attending the meeting is steadily increasing (not the average age of its membership, but of Friends actually attending), that's an indication that the meeting has entered the later phases of the life cycle. Usually, such a meeting will stop replacing its younger generations as they mature or move away. If the average age of attenders is steadily increasing, then we can say the meeting is also aging. It will be necessary to reevaluate the meeting's structure and make some changes simply because aging Friends—even though they have much to give spiritually—will eventually have less physical energy to spare.

Can we carry out the basic functions of a Quaker meeting? A healthy Quaker meeting is capable of accepting new members, conducting marriages, holding memorial meetings, and making essential decisions through corporate discernment. If the faith community cannot do those things (or suspects it could not do those things if asked), it is already not functioning as a Quaker meeting. It is almost certainly time to consider laying the meeting down or at least to consider restructuring into a worship group under another meeting's care.

Institutional Adaptations

Quaker process can be a confusing thing. It's confusing, first of all, because it is not singular. "Good Quaker process" in one meeting or region is quite different from "good Quaker process" in another, and yet each group tends to speak as though the local way is the only way. It's also confusing for newcomers, who do not understand the functions of individual committees or how to suggest new items of business. The situation is even worse in meetings where systems are complicated but not written down or where the actual system differs from the official one.

But Quaker process is also comforting. Those who understand it and are practiced in using it find it predictable, controllable, and safe. We tend to talk about "Quaker process" as though it is a sacred thing. I would venture that it's not—not if what we mean by "Quaker process" is the committee structures, our ways of forming agendas, our habits to do with approving minutes, who reports to business meetings in which month of the year, and how we obtain the clerk's permission to speak. All of these practices are part of the institution. They can and should be changed to suit the needs of a changing community.

What is, in fact, sacred is Friends' theological understandings, the spiritual truths we have discerned over many generations as a community. These include beliefs like ready access to the Holy Spirit and the need for big decisions to be discerned in group settings. They include the practices of truth-telling and other forms of integrity, living in that life and power that takes away the occasion for war, recognizing that of God in each person and treating them accordingly, and understanding ourselves in relationship with a much broader body of Friends (and the wider church). These are just a few examples of spiritual truths. There are many others.

Institutional Adaptations

This matters because, as we consider institutional adaptations, we must be able to differentiate between *how* we do things and *why* we do things. The "how" is procedural, institutional, and changeable, stemming mostly from the habits and the convenience of people who came before us. The "why" is spiritual and generally eternal, stemming from God's revelations over a long period of time.

God probably does not require the Ministry and Counsel Committee to meet on second Tuesdays at 7 p.m. At some point, we chose second Tuesdays at 7 p.m, probably because this timing allowed all the members of the committee to attend. That's the underlying spiritual truth—the fact that the meetings should be accessible to all the committee members. Second Tuesdays at 7 p.m is just a habit. We should probably switch to third Wednesdays at 10am if, years later, that is the time that will make it more possible for all members of the committee to participate.

We can actually take this another step further. God probably does not require us to have a Ministry and Counsel Committee. At some point, we constituted a Ministry and Counsel Committee, probably because we needed some designated group of people to take responsibility for arranging worship and providing care of the meeting members. That's the underlying spiritual truth—our call to worship and to provide mutual care. If having a Ministry and Counsel Committee is no longer serving that purpose, we should probably try something different.

It's time to delve into that "something different." I've been speaking about the life cycle of meetings, about institutional mismatch in changing communities, about assessing and naming the community's condition, and about how we might consider changes, but I haven't yet offered examples of such changes. You'll find those in the paragraphs below. Each example is explored more deeply later in this book. For now, it's important to know that a meeting might be called to any of these possibilities, or to more than one of them, or to something in between. A faith community does not need to choose between the status quo and laying down the meeting. There are many ways forward that may be appropriate.

Changing the committee structure. In some cases, a meeting needs to overhaul its committee structure, which is too large and too complicated for the actual condition of the community now. Such meetings might explore using working groups, task groups, volunteer roles, and other creative pathways toward getting the work done in a manner that better fits the size of the faith community and the individuals in it.

Staff transitions. As a meeting moves into later stages of its life cycle, it will reach a point when it needs to reassess its staff structure. This may involve reducing the number of staff or shifting full-time positions to part-time positions. In a few cases, the appropriate response for an aging meeting is the opposite: it's hiring more staff. In all cases, the changes must be made with an eye to economic fairness and good employment practices. We can also be guided by paying attention to the meeting's callings and its members' spiritual gifts.

Hybrid meetings and online meetings. In the modern era, new use of the internet is sometimes the faithful response for a changing meeting. But this is not only a technological change. Becoming a hybrid or online meeting has many implications for the faith community.

Combining or merging meetings. Sometimes a meeting responds to change by either merging directly with another meeting or by coming under the care of another meeting. Any form of combining is an adjustment for all concerned, but it's sometimes the best way to address property problems, shrinking attendance, or demographic changes in the neighborhood community.

Restructuring the meeting. In some cases, a monthly meeting should no longer be a monthly meeting. It might consider becoming a preparative meeting, an executive meeting, a worship group, or a house church. This option is most likely to be helpful for a meeting that has deep worship but that either doesn't feel called to all the business of a monthly meeting or is no longer capable of keeping up with it.

Changing property relationships. Most often, this will mean selling a building, but it can also involve rental agreements, property-sharing, land-marking, sale of air rights, and a number of other creative solutions. The appropriate way forward will depend on the circumstances of the meeting (financially and energetically) and also on the circumstances of the neighborhood.

Laying down the meeting. Eventually, every meeting will close. The questions about laying down a meeting are not about whether it should happen but whether now is the appropriate time. Just as humans can prepare for death before the actual event, meetings—if they start while the meeting is still healthy enough to do so—can make certain decisions about property and assets, care for members, and preservation of historical records well before the final day comes.

Why Adapting Is Hard

MOST MEETINGS HAVE TROUBLE adapting their institutional structures. Because change in the meeting community happens so slowly, it might be hard to recognize that we have a problem. If we do recognize the problem, we may hope it will go away on its own. And if we do acknowledge a need to make changes, we may disagree about how we need to change and when.

A few specific sources of resistance tend to rise predictably in changing meetings. Each is part of our normal human ways of interacting with the world and not especially blameworthy. But they're worth listing here so we can recognize them in ourselves and in others and work through them.

Gradualism (especially loops and spirals). I've mentioned several times that it's difficult for Friends to recognize new stages of a meeting life cycle because the transitions happen so gradually. I've also said that no meeting proceeds neatly from one stage to the next. Instead, we tend to have periods of growth and activity and periods of stasis or shrinking throughout the life cycle.

Sometimes, Friends see these swings up and down and interpret what's happening to the meeting as a loop. We say, "Our meeting has always had times when it grows and times when it shrinks. Right now, we're in a shrinking time, but it's a loop. We'll start growing again."

It may or may not be true that we'll start growing again, but the bigger problem is seeing a loop when what we really have is a spiral. The word "loop" would describe a meeting with attendance like this:

Before the Resurrection

1990	120 Friends at worship
1995	80 Friends at worship
2000	123 Friends at worship
2005	84 Friends at worship
2010	117 Friends at worship
2015	79 Friends at worship
2020	125 Friends at worship

The actual attendance pattern at many meetings can be better described as a "spiral," like this:

1990	120 Friends at worship
1995	80 Friends at worship
2000	113 Friends at worship
2005	73 Friends at worship
2010	100 Friends at worship
2015	64 Friends at worship
2020	78 Friends at worship

You can see that in the second table, the so-called high attendance in 2020 is actually lower than the so-called low attendance in 1995. This is not a loop, it's a spiral, in which each high is progressively lower than the last high, and the overall pattern is still one of shrinking numbers. Spirals are especially difficult to perceive when the numbers are relatively small (ranging, for example, from 8 to 16 rather than 64 to 120). But they're also difficult to perceive if most Friends in the meeting haven't been attending for multiple decades and if no one is tracking quantitative data.

A meeting in a spiral does need to make some institutional adaptations to better suit its smaller community, but the spiral pattern can make it very tempting to believe that the problem will simply solve itself if we wait a few years. And conditions may improve somewhat—but the committee structure will still be too complex, the building too expensive, and so forth.

Source-of-value confusion. When we adjust the institution to better match the changing community, we almost always eliminate roles. This can be emotionally hard on a Friend who is deriving his source of value from a particular role. For example, imagine a Quaker meeting with a building that's over a hundred years old. It's in poor repair, and the boiler has a disheartening tendency to stop working about forty-five minutes before worship. One member of the meeting seems to have a magic touch with this boiler. He can go down to the basement, wrestle with it for a few minutes, and emerge a hero. The rest of us praise him every time this happens.

In such circumstances, it can be very easy for our Friend to think his source of value to the community is based on his ability to fix the boiler. Similar things can happen with a Friend who's been making the bulletin for thirty years, or the Friend who's been serving as recording clerk, or the Friend who makes apple pie for the potluck. If we suspect we are of value to the community primarily because of a role we inhabit, we will almost automatically resist any change that threatens to take that role away.

The best remedy for this phenomenon is prevention, and it's never too late to start. We can make a practice of letting every Friend know—young, old, new, familiar—that we value them primarily for the people they are, not for the work they do. The culture of our community will influence the best way of doing this, but possibilities range from just-thinking-of-you cards to verbal affirmation to invitations to dinner. Each of us needs to feel as though we have connections in the community that go much deeper than our service to it.

Saviorism. This is related to source-of-value confusion, but it's a distinct phenomenon. Sometimes, one Friend or a small group of Friends can see that there aren't enough people to get the necessary work done, and they begin to over-function—to work as hard as they can, or sometimes harder than they can in the long term—in order to keep things going. There is nothing inherently wrong with this reaction, especially because we often perceive the problem as short-term.

But when the problem turns out to be a long-term problem, it's not right to leave a few Friends working themselves to exhaustion. Aside from our care for those individuals, there is a spiritual truth at stake, the need for Friends in the meeting to share in the work. This sharing doesn't need to be equal, exactly, but it should happen in measures appropriate to each person's capacity, and that simply isn't possible if an inappropriately large institutional structure must be managed by too few people.

Friends who have been over-functioning may be tired and hyper-focused. "Once we've done such-and-such, the situation will improve." If they are thinking, internally, that their actions will rescue the meeting—will get it through a difficult but temporary phase—then a collective move toward significant change can feel like a betrayal. The internal thought process might go like this: "I've been working so hard on getting us through this, and now the meeting is saying that I've wasted my time. Where have they all been, anyway, while I've been doing all the work to keep us going? They don't understand the situation. I can do this if they just stop fighting me."

There is only one Savior, and none of us is Jesus. The truth is, most Friends in a savior position cannot rescue the meeting long-term. And if they could, would it be the right thing to do? A Quaker meeting is meant to be a collective effort, in which we practice mutual service and mutual support. If the community as a whole is no longer able to continue work at the previous institutional scale, the faithful response is probably to adapt the institution to something smaller and simpler so that we can return to collective discernment and cooperative work. After all, the practice of working together is the underlying spiritual truth that we are trying to live.

Responsibility to literal or spiritual ancestors. "What about the people who came before us? They established this meeting. They built this building. Shouldn't we keep it going for them?" I have heard this said word-for-word in multiple conversations, and there's something very beautiful about the Friend whose drive is to honor the Friends who came before.

Our ancestors' work is never wasted. Aside from the fruits of the work itself, we receive their wisdom by way of tradition. In the corporate discernment process, tradition is the contribution of the dead. We've inherited practices, property, beliefs, stories, and rituals. Which of these are we called to preserve?

Friends believe in continuing revelation. We know that God will tell us more, will guide us in this particular moment, if we only listen. It would seem very unusual for God to tell us to reject everything that we received from our ancestors, but most of the time, that's not what we're doing, even if we sell our property or lay down the meeting. Most of the time, we will discover that God's call for our ancestors looked a certain way because that was what God needed done in that particular time and place. Our call will be different, appropriate for our time and place. To adapt or even to end the meeting is not dishonoring the work that came before us. It is taking what we have learned from our ancestors and asking God how God would like us to apply it. What does it mean to be faithful now?

Responsibility to a theoretical future. Some Friends wonder if the meeting needs to continue as-is just in case seekers arrive sometime down the road. Those of us who have, ourselves, been seekers are especially conscious of the need to be accessible. But we do not know what these theoretical future seekers will need. I would say it's unlikely they'll need a meeting with an institutional structure that's large and unwieldy. If we become a house church or move to a rental property or reduce our committees, we can still be found, and the smaller and more flexible community may be exactly what seekers are looking for. And if we lay down the meeting, we can trust that God will raise a new one up if one is needed. That might be what our resurrection looks like.

Confusing concerns with leadings. We are God's hands and feet on earth, but we do not have an infinite number of hands, and God does not expect us to do everything. This is why Quakers distinguish between concerns and leadings. A concern is a deep spiritual knowing that something must be done, while a leading is the spiritual prompting to do it. Many of us carry more concerns than leadings. When we confuse a concern with a leading, we try to do things that God has not asked us to do and that we may not be equipped to do. This is one form of what Friends call "outrunning our Guide." An individual Friend or a meeting might resist doing less because we feel the work is too important to lay down. But the question is not whether the work is important. The question is whether God is asking *us*, *now*, to do *this* work in *this* way. If not, we might pray that God will send some other group to do it.

Love of the familiar. When God called Abram to the promised land, he first required that Abram leave his father's house. It was a command to abandon the familiar. We often love what is familiar. Even if we don't—even if the status quo makes us deeply uncomfortable—it's at least a situation we understand. The journey to the promised land takes us across brand new territory, and we have no way of knowing what to expect.

One normal reaction to this kind of journey is grief. An institutional adaptation in a meeting will often bring grief. We know from experience that grief is complicated, with many moving and unpredictable parts, including sadness and anger and resistance. A community in transition may experience all of these, and unfortunately, the members of that community will not all experience each emotional state at the same time. Working through our emotional responses to change is such a significant part of the institutional adaptation process that you'll find much more about it later in this book.

The Process of Adapting

How do we get from here to there, especially when we don't know where we're going? Friends know that receiving guidance is about deep listening, but the process of institutional adaptations can be so complicated that a map might be helpful.

The pathway may look something like this:

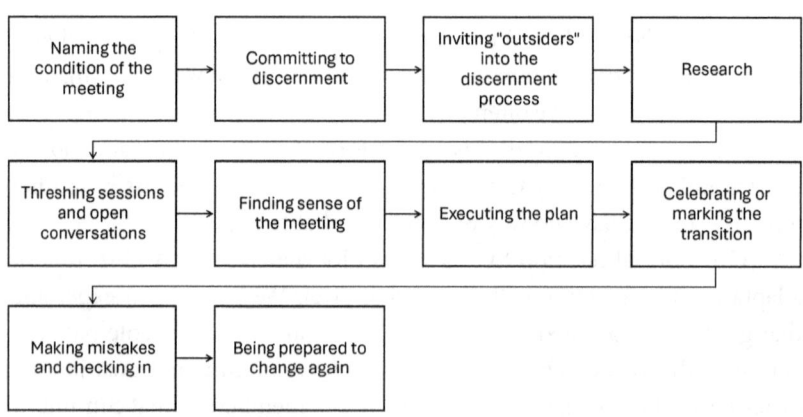

Like any other diagram, this one oversimplifies. A meeting's actual process will move in fits and starts, and it's not essential that the steps go in precisely this order, although there are some things that shouldn't be skipped. The diagram above is relevant regardless of the type of institutional adaptation you're making. Some adaptations are more difficult than others, but whether you're selling your building, redesigning your committee system, or laying down the meeting, you'll go through essentially the same beginning, middle, and end.

Naming the condition of the meeting. This is the step in which we say, "Our institutional system is no longer helping our community to be faithful." We can say that in a lot of ways. We can use queries to help support this naming, or it might come from open worship, or it might be something stated at coffee hour. An individual can be the first to name the meeting's condition, but it's unlikely much more can happen unless a majority of regular attenders agree that the meeting has a problem—though Friends might not agree yet what the problem is.

Most often, a meeting enters this step when it feels forced to do so by circumstance. The meeting has a shortage of people to do the work, or a shortage of money to cover necessary expenses, or both. Sometimes the naming happens before or after a major conflict. Friends might be generally unhappy at the time of naming, but I've also seen it arise as a very calm, very spiritually grounded recognition of change in a group that's ready to hear and affirm it.

Meetings with an excess of money might have an especially hard time noticing a structural mismatch. Some meetings have extraordinary endowments and investment portfolios, so they can easily cover their expenses for years or decades even if the meeting's property and ministries are no longer appropriate for the present worshipping community. A meeting with an excess of money can hire extra staff, as much as is needed, to keep things going when the meeting members themselves can't take responsibility for the day-to-day work.

The lack of practical pressure to make a change can cause such a meeting to defer decisions indefinitely. It might be worth asking: what are we, as a community, led to do at this time? Is it God's will that our financial assets be devoted to perpetuating this system? Might we be led differently if we take time to listen?

Committing to discernment. This may seem like an obvious step, perhaps too obvious to bother mentioning. But something funny happens when Friends are trying to figure out next steps related to institutional structures, especially if the discernment involves disbursement of money, selling of property, or significant restructuring of the meeting. We may be overwhelmed by possibilities. We may have the opposite problem and struggle to imagine any acceptable solution. We may have strong emotions and not know how or when to express them.

The meeting as a whole must commit to corporate discernment as the pathway forward. "We will listen for God's leading together, and when we have found it, we will follow it." This does not mean that every individual will necessarily be satisfied with the final result, because corporate discernment is not a consensus process. It means, though, that no small group can rush ahead, nor can any individual or small group prevent action in the long-term. Committing to corporate discernment means trusting the community's discernment over our own.

Some groups will discover, in the process of committing to corporate discernment, that not everyone in the group is clear on what that means. Individuals may not understand what is expected of them. This happens most often in meetings with a large proportion of newcomers, but even meetings with mostly experienced Friends might discover they've become complacent and have lost some understanding about Friends' spiritual practices. In that case, the meeting will need to stop and do some religious education before trying to move forward. A group that does not fully understand corporate discernment, or that is not fully committed, cannot attempt to use that process to make big and potentially contentious decisions.

The other useful step here is to identify Friends who will pray for the meeting. This is not limited to asking Friends to serve as elders or prayerful presences during gatherings, although that practice is useful. Community members who are gifted intercessors might pray throughout the week—for Friends' faithfulness, wisdom, patience, truth-telling, courage, and anything else that's needed.

Inviting "outsiders" to the discernment process. The meeting discerns its own future. That said, there are times when it can be helpful to invite someone from outside the meeting to join the conversation. This person could be another Friend from the region or the yearly meeting. They might be a staff member or clerk of some larger Quaker body or might be a traveling minister. A Friend from outside the meeting can facilitate large group conversations, can connect the meeting to resources it might not otherwise know about, can listen in one-on-one and small group settings as Friends process their emotional reactions, and can mediate conflict. Such a Friend might even clerk a business meeting so that the clerk of the meeting can step out of that role and participate as a member of the body.

Not every meeting will need such an outsider, and the outsider won't be a superstar or a miracle worker. But this outsider Friend (or group of outsider Friends) will care about the people in the meeting and ideally have some relevant skill set. They can be very helpful in terms of providing a slightly removed perspective and taking some of the pressure off Friends in service roles within the meeting.

It will also be important to contact another group of Friends. This group isn't really "outsiders." It's Friends who consider themselves part of the meeting but who have not participated in a long time, most often because of geographic separation. Distant members, young adults who grew up in the meeting, and living Friends who were married under the care of the meeting should be contacted as soon as possible if the meeting is considering significant change. They will need opportunities to respond to proposals, express their feelings about the situation, and participate in some way in marking the transition.

Corporate discernment generally requires Friends to be in the room (or the electronic "room") during the worshipful gathering. This is because we experience collective spiritual change during corporate discernment. But there is no reason why distant or absent Friends could not send letters or video clips or some other contribution to be considered. These should be shared at the beginning of the gathering and can be used to inform Friends' discernment but cannot dictate the results of that discernment. The most important factor is the guidance of Spirit in the time spent together in worship.

Research. This really occurs before, during, and after the corporate discernment process. One group that has research to do is trustees or buildings and grounds committees. If the meeting is considering restructuring, laying itself down, or changing its relationship with its property, there will be legal questions to address. Laws will differ based on the meeting's location and on the existing legal status of the meeting, and it's important to pay attention to both restrictions and opportunities dictated by relevant law.

Recording clerks and historians may also have research to do. When the meeting is discerning its next steps, it can help to know what Friends in previous years or previous generations have had to say about God's calling. For example, if a meeting is considering what to do with a large endowment that is no longer needed, guidance might be found in old minutes—either about the donor's intent or about what the meeting discerned at the time regarding its use.

Clerks and pastors and ministry and council committee members might research the yearly meeting's book of discipline, discovering what it has to say about the process of institutional adaptations of local groups. If the book of discipline does not provide useful guidance, or if the yearly meeting doesn't have a book of discipline at all, these Friends might contact other faith communities in similar situations to discover what examples might be available there.

Threshing sessions and open conversations. A formal business meeting is the best setting for finding sense of the meeting, but it may not be the best setting for Friends to work through grief or ask logistical questions.

If what's needed is a chance to simply express thoughts or feelings out loud—without direct responses from anyone and without a need to make an immediate decision—then a threshing session might be the best match. This is a gathering for extended unprogrammed (open) worship in which each Friend is encouraged to rise (once) and express whatever is on their heart. Threshing sessions also help us to understand one another more deeply in terms of the particular issue at hand.

If what's needed is an opportunity to talk through logistics, a simple Q&A or conversation over sandwiches might be best. Sometimes Friends need the chance to talk about what might happen to the peace committee, or who will keep the hymnals, or whether it's possible to wait on making a final decision until after Theresa and Ken's marriage. Not all such questions need to happen in a worshipful meeting for business session. An informal conversational setting can actually help this sort of thing happen more efficiently—but it's important that someone makes sure the conversation doesn't drift into the kind of decision-making better done in a formal meeting for business.

In still other cases, Friends in the meeting need a structured way to consider detailed problems or proposals. An informal conversation isn't enough because it will wander off track, but a formal meeting for business or threshing session can't support the complexity of the issues. This is a great time to bring in an external facilitator who can craft an approach including speaking and listening, worship and prayer, explanations and diagrams, and other creative approaches. Such a gathering can often prepare Friends to enter formal corporate discernment with a stronger understanding of the questions at hand.

Finding sense of the meeting. This is the moment when we become clear about our collective next steps. It might actually happen several times during an adaptation process—first, when we have sense of the meeting to ask a task group to research real estate sales in our neighborhood; second, when we have sense of the meeting to allow the buildings and grounds committee to hire a realtor; third, when we have sense of the meeting to sell at less than market value to the Presbyterians. Finding sense of the meeting is not necessarily an act of finding total agreement about what's best. Instead, it's the act of becoming clear about what the group as a whole perceives as God's will for us. I, as an individual, do not have to agree with that perception; I only have to be clear that it's the group's perception, and I trust the group.

We may find sense of the meeting unexpectedly quickly. We may also find sense of the meeting unexpectedly slowly. Sometimes it will sneak up on us in a moment when we didn't think we'd find it.

There are two things we should be wary of. One is finding sense of the meeting of the day when Joe just happens to be absent. Friends do believe that corporate discernment is done by those who are present, but if Joe is our beloved Friend and we know he has concerns about the plan, it is probably best not to affirm the plan right after his emergency appendectomy. This is a violation of trust that will have a serious impact on the community.

The other is making sure we really have found sense of the meeting. Someone—usually the clerk, but not always—should attempt to articulate the sense of the meeting. "I believe that what I've heard us say is. . ." Some groups of Friends approve a written minute before leaving the meeting so that there is no doubt what we've agreed upon. If that's not in keeping with a group's tradition, there should at least be a repeated articulation of the plan and a chance for everyone present to approve or object. We need to be sure that no one will go out to the parking lot with an attitude of, "That might be what got said in the meeting, but I think it'd be better if we did things a bit differently. I'll just make sure that my idea is what gets presented when we meet with the bank. . ."

Executing the plan. Once we've discerned sense of the meeting, we move ahead and put that sense into practice. This is the step in which we disband half of our committees, or merge the two meetings, or formally put the building on the market. It's unlikely to go perfectly smoothly. Some transitions necessarily take time, so there's a delay—a sort of waiting period—between the decision and the completion of the action. We also might encounter complications, like an unanticipated legal snag or the sudden illness of a person who was important to our next steps. This can be frustrating but isn't usually an indication that we've discerned incorrectly. Sometimes things just don't work out as planned.

Celebrating or marking the transition. Early Friends rejected external sacraments. They believed that the physical sacrament itself was unnecessary because sacraments (such as baptism and communion) happened internally, invisibly, and spiritually as part of worship.

Some Friends' meetings still resist ceremonies and rituals of all kinds. There are certainly cases in which this might be rightly led. If the meeting is clear that not marking an institutional transition in any way is a matter of Spirit-led conscience, the meeting should not do so. But in most cases, an event to honor the change will be useful.

If the meeting is being laid down, or if the meeting is selling its building, Friends might hold a memorial meeting. This is an opportunity for those gathered to share their memories about the community or about the physical space. If two meetings are merging, they might each bring some physical object that is representative of their history and put them together in the center of the worship space. If committees are being laid down, the Friends who are serving or have served on those committees might stand to be recognized or share a particularly fond memory about their service.

Making mistakes and checking in. Almost no transition will proceed flawlessly. Perhaps there were four parts to our agreed-upon plan. Three work out well; one does not unfold as anticipated and causes conflict; and there's a fifth thing we didn't think of and probably should have. This does not mean that our discernment was wrong or that we've been unfaithful. It means that we did the best we could discerning next steps, but God will probably provide additional guidance if we listen again, to God and to one another.

We need a regular practice of checking in with each other: "Is this way of doing things working for you? Do you think we're still on the right track?" Some communities create formal assessment processes for one year or two years or five years in the future. There's nothing wrong with this. But it's important, too, for us to pay attention when somebody tells us they're struggling over lemon squares at social hour. If things aren't working out for everyone, we can sometimes make a small and relatively informal tweak to make it better. Not everything requires starting over. What's crucial is learning from each new step.

Being prepared to adapt again. The community will continue to change. Friends will age or move away. New Friends will appear. An economic crisis will cause financial shortfall. The neighborhood demographics will shift. When we go through the work of institutional adaptation, we might feel like we've earned a rest and resist adapting again for quite a while. But just

The Process of Adapting

as the previous institutional structure wasn't appropriate forever, the new institutional structure also won't be appropriate forever.

The question to ask in each new moment is, "How can we most faithfully respond to God's call for us in this time and this place?"

For Clerks of Local Meetings

GENERALLY SPEAKING, CLERKS ARE an organizational force within a Quaker meeting. At a minimum, they facilitate meetings for business, but they often end up being a *de facto* executive officer of a meeting—the person to whom everyone complains, and the person who deals with things that nobody else is assigned to deal with.

One responsibility of clerks is to shepherd a meeting through institutional adaptations. This is rarely in the clerk's job description or meeting handbook, but it happens by default because it is no one else's responsibility. This is not to say that the clerk *leads* the meeting through the process. The meeting discerns its own future. Rather, the clerk *shepherds* the meeting through the process as an organizational force caring for the sense of the meeting.

Individuals approach the clerk role in different ways, according to spiritual gifts and personalities. Four models are described below. Any given clerk may resonate with more than one model, but it's likely that some will be a better description than others. These different types of clerks will approach transitions differently.

Train conductors. For these clerks, organization is like breathing. It's fairly easy to track a lot of details. This clerk knows which committees are functioning and which are not, starts gatherings on time and ends them on time, keeps Friends on topic, and carries forward to the next month anything left unfinished on the agenda. During institutional adaptations, their strength is in the discernment, research, and execution phases because of their affinity for detail. But they might struggle with naming the condition of the meeting because their focus is so much on making things work as they are. They might also naturally over-function, which can obscure the actual condition of the meeting.

People-tenders. For these clerks, nothing overshadows the wellbeing of individual Friends. They know who is ill or celebrating a graduation or looking for a job. They start and end gatherings at the time that seems right for the group's emotional or spiritual state, and when they follow up with people after the meeting, it's less likely to be "have you finished your assignment?" and more likely to be "how are you feeling about your assignment?" During institutional adaptations, their strength is in naming the condition of the meeting, threshing sessions, and checking in with everyone. But they might struggle to provide an organizational structure and keep the process moving step by step. They might also lose track of details or follow-up because their focus is so much more on people than institutional minutiae.

Cupholders. For these clerks, what matters is the community as a whole. They take very little initiative. They approach everything, even things like creating an agenda or deciding whether to start or end a business meeting, as a collective decision. They show very little attachment (although they might feel attachment internally) to any particular decision or the consequences of any particular decision. They believe the most important thing is giving space for the community to guide itself. During institutional adaptations, their strength is flexibility. They will not nudge the community toward any decision, which leaves absolute freedom for innovation. But they also won't provide any guidance or insist on follow-up, which can allow the community to relax back into the status quo.

Vision-casters. For these clerks, a better future calls. They are constantly considering the possibilities. They will incorporate readings and queries into gatherings and will add space for broadly envisioning the future into agendas. They see Friends' potential and might be very good at affirming and drawing out spiritual gifts. During institutional adaptations, their strength is in naming the condition of the meeting and providing ongoing motivation to the group. But they may not have a deep understanding of how the institution can support the new vision, and sometimes they can push too hard and forget to allow the community to discern its own future.

These are four very general profiles and shouldn't be used as a diagnostic test. There's also nothing inherently wrong or right about any of the four. But having a rough sense of these types can help clerks anticipate what kind of help they may need, especially during institutional adaptations.

Train conductors may need to identify and learn from Friends in the meeting who are good at pastoral care. People-tenders may need an assistant clerk or recording clerk who's especially good at tracking detail. Cupholders may need to recognize which Friends are organizationally minded and pay attention to their suggestions to keep the process going. And vision-casters may need regular conversations with someone who can help them find a balance in terms of how hard to push the group so that they can inspire but not bully.

What is the role of the clerk when a meeting is going through significant change?

First, the local meeting clerk has a unique, though not necessarily superior, understanding of the condition of the meeting. Other Friends are likely to be focused on the work of particular committees or other relatively narrow forms of service. They may have an in-depth understanding of the work they are doing, but the clerk's perception of the meeting's condition will be broad even if it's shallow. For this reason, the clerk is more likely to notice overarching patterns, such as multiple committees struggling to function or budget lines going unspent or illness and exhaustion among members. The clerk might find opportunities to articulate these patterns for the meeting: "I have a sense that most of our committees are struggling." Or, "It seems as though we've had a budget shortfall several years in a row."

Clerks have to be careful, of course, about how and when they articulate these things because the clerk does not dictate next steps for the meeting or try to prod the meeting toward a particular decision. The trick is to name what's true at a moment when the group seems able to hear it—but gently and with spaciousness for the possibility that the clerk's perception is wrong. Another strategy is to check in with individual members of the community, asking about their own sense of how things are going, though it's important that this not be done in a way that can be viewed as keeping secrets from the group as a whole.

Once the meeting has named its condition—"our institutional structure is no longer supporting our community"—the clerk will need to ask for next steps. "If we agree this is where we are, what shall we do about it?" Sometimes Friends will be ready to name next steps right away. Usually, those next steps will have something to do with additional conversation, research, or appointing a task group.

Occasionally, a meeting will name its condition and then be reluctant to do anything at all. In these cases, a clerk might offer some multiple-choice options: "We could talk about this again next month, or we could ask for someone to come up with a set of proposals, or. . ." If the meeting is still unable to affirm a next step, it may simply need time to absorb the situation before acting, and the clerk can name that.

Other times, one or more Friends will leap directly to making suggestions for solving the meeting's problems. Even if these suggestions are good ones, the meeting as a whole may not be ready to affirm them yet. A clerk can gently recommend that Friends focus on how to explore the issues more deeply for now and not try to solve them right away. This prevents the group from becoming divided.

When the meeting is in the process of change—by which I mean doing research, having threshing sessions, considering possible solutions, and so forth—the clerk can move into a pace-setting role. Generally speaking, a clerk can pose questions and place items on the agenda in a way that is thoughtful about the speed of change, which ideally will move slightly faster than the most deliberate Friends find comfortable but slightly slower than the most innovative Friends find satisfying. Sometimes, the meeting will need a reset in the middle of a months-long discernment process, and it will demonstrate this with emotional flare-ups, lots of missed deadlines, or extreme difficulty in finding sense of the meeting. When this happens, the clerk might recommend a break (a month or two without action), a special worship session, a day of fun community-building activities, or some combination thereof. Again, it's the meeting that affirms these possibilities or doesn't. The clerk can only suggest.

Clerking a meeting through major change means shepherding a community of people. It's a challenging task, and this is where it's good to remember the strengths and weaknesses of different types of clerks. A vision-caster might struggle with pacing and with releasing control over sense of the meeting. A cupholder might lean on an assistant clerk to structure conversations. A people-tender might need help finding the right next concrete steps to suggest, and a train conductor may slip too easily into technical details and forget about the humans. No clerk needs to do the work alone. It's always possible to reach out to other Friends in the meeting.

The clerk also has some responsibility for paying attention to execution. When Friends have done very difficult discernment, we sometimes feel such relief at affirming a minute that we feel finished and fail to follow through. In these moments, a local meeting clerk can look back at the minutes from the most recent meeting and check in with Friends. Has the building and grounds committee made that phone call yet? Is the new volunteer form up and running?

Finally, it's the local meeting clerk who can remember the need for ongoing evaluation. We don't make a change once and then assume that will be our new form forever. We need to listen to one another, pay attention to the impact of our decisions, and adjust as necessary. Clerks can facilitate that through private conversations or by giving time on agendas for such reflection. "How is it going? Is there anything we need to talk about again?"

For Pastors

QUAKER PASTORS ARE IN an unusual position theologically and structurally (as Quaker pastors already know). They have influence, but not authority. They have responsibilities, but not absolute power. They care for the community and sometimes lead it, in a way, but more like a sheepdog than a workplace boss. Quaker pastors are often underpaid or bivocational and not infrequently blamed for things that aren't their fault. They are released ministers—members of the community that are offered financial support so that they can practice their gifts more fully within the meeting.

Just like clerks, Quaker pastors are likely to perceive the condition of the whole body, but they must be careful about how and when they name this. A Quaker pastor fills a prophetic role but also a healing role and a teaching role and an exhortation role and pastoral care role. God invites the Quaker pastor to listen very deeply, which is the only way a pastor can know which type of presence is required moment to moment.

The pastor is not the only one who can name the condition of the meeting. Naming can come from the clerk, from a trustee, from a recording clerk, or from any other person in the community. But sometimes, the pastor will feel called to say it: "Our institutional structure is no longer supporting our community."

Because a Quaker pastor has influence but not authority, the Quaker pastor can only do what a pre-existing trust relationship allows. The pastor isn't solely responsible for the level of pre-existing trust; the members of the meeting also influence this. But to exceed the boundaries of that trust, whatever boundaries those may be, can damage the relationship between pastor and meeting and can lead to an adversarial relationship, which further limits the pastor's ability to serve the community.

In some cases, the meeting is deeply trusting of the pastor. Other times, most members of the meeting are apathetic about institutional structures. In these situations, it would be very easy for the pastor to become the driving force behind change. We have to remind ourselves that *the meeting discerns its own future*. This basic theological principle is at the heart of Quaker practice, and if the meeting sells its building or lays itself down or restructures or merges with another meeting mostly because the pastor thinks it's a good idea, we've given up something precious. We've also quite possibly taken the wrong steps forward, since Friends believe that genuine corporate discernment is more likely to reflect God's will than the discernment of any individual.

The opposite situation can happen, as well. If the meeting does not trust the pastor, or if members of the meeting feel it is inappropriate for the pastor to have a role in structural change, Friends may push back reflexively to anything the pastor seems to be suggesting. So it falls upon the pastor to be very careful indeed.

The pastor has a few specific tools that can help a community moving through change: the message, the "pastor voice," and pastoral care.

When the pastor is conscious of the condition of the meeting, a prepared message can reflect and respond to that. If Friends are tired, frustrated, angry, or grieving, a message is an ideal way to affirm and honor those feelings. What's special about a message given in worship is that it doesn't have to be literal. Pastors can use stories and scriptures and metaphors, and that distance from the specifics of the work Friends are doing can help a lot in providing a new perspective.

A pastor also has the "pastor voice" in committee meetings and conversations. The pastor will always be heard differently from other members of the meeting and in some communities will be given a small measure of deference. For this reason, the pastor voice must be used judiciously. But it can be very helpful, especially if the meeting is feeling stuck, for the pastor to offer a well-timed question or new insight, especially if the insight is grounded in the history of the meeting community.

Pastoral care is always part of the pastor's work, but during times of transitions, there will be additional opportunities for walking alongside. Some Friends will be concerned that the meeting is changing too fast. Others will believe it is changing too slowly. In both cases, having someone to talk to may allow for emotional venting. A pastor can also help Friends become clear on whether their concerns need to be shared broadly and, if so, how to express those concerns in a manner that is respectful and well-defined.

A third category of Friends will simply be grieving. Any change can cause grief as we step away from our old way of being, but we don't often acknowledge this in our society. Friends will understand grief for a lost person or perhaps a lost job or lost home but may have trouble recognizing and processing grief for a changing committee structure or renting out the meetinghouse. Sometimes grief needs to be named and prayed over.

The pastor will nearly always have a role in marking the meeting's transition. If a meeting is laying itself down or selling a building, it might hold a memorial meeting. If a meeting is merging with another meeting or restructuring into a different form of faith community, it might have a special worship gathering to mark the first Sunday in the new configuration.

Pastors experience one other type of stress during institutional transitions. Usually, only the pastor—no other community member—faces potential loss of a job, or a shift from full-time to part-time work, as part of the change. Not every Quaker meeting excludes pastors from the corporate discernment regarding whether to make such changes. Depending on how the local meeting conducts business, the pastor might have to affirm sense of the meeting for the loss of the paid pastoral role.

Like everyone else, the pastor must trust the discernment of the community over their own individual judgment. It can be extremely difficult not to advocate for the continuation of one's own livelihood. The pastor will need some person outside the meeting with whom to speak about the situation and work through their own emotional and spiritual concerns so that these do not prevent the pastor from engaging appropriately with the meeting during the transition. This confidant could be another pastor, a staff member or clerk from a regional or yearly meeting, a mental health professional, or even a good friend, as long as that person is not part of the meeting community and can be relied upon not to gossip.

For Record Keepers

THE TERM "RECORD KEEPER" isn't part of Friends' usual vocabulary. I'm talking collectively about statisticians, recording clerks, recorders, historians, treasurers, bookkeepers, archivists, newsletter editors, and website managers.[1] These are the Friends who are paying attention to the data and the stories of the meeting. They create and preserve the story of how we have responded together to God's leadings.

Some types of record keepers (statisticians, recorders, treasurers, bookkeepers) make quantitative records. These Friends may pay attention to membership statistics, attendance at worship, community members impacted by meeting ministries, number of visitors each week, budgets and financial reports, and individual Friends' giving patterns.

Other types of record keepers (recording clerks, newsletter editors, website managers) create narrative records. These Friends tell the stories of the meeting now, mostly in words but sometimes in pictures. They publish announcements, make note of important decisions, and create written reflections of what is happening in the faith community.

Still other record keepers (historians, archivists) preserve and interpret the past records of the meeting. These Friends see and read and hear the old stories and make sure they'll be available for future generations. They file documents, ask questions about what older Friends can remember, and find ways to make the historical narrative accessible.

Collectively, record keepers have an enormous role to play in institutional change. First, they are well-positioned to notice patterns. If numbers are dropping (in worship attendance, contributions to the meeting, visitors,

---

1. None of these terms has an agreed-upon definition that all Friends understand. For the purposes of this section, you may have to do some mental translation.

etc.), the record keepers are the ones who have this information. They can report such trends to the meeting. It helps if such a report is accompanied by a strong query. For example: what is the impact of fewer Friends at meeting for worship? What does it tell us about our community that the average individual contribution to the meeting has dropped by 45 percent? Is our meeting budget still an accurate reflection of God's call for our community? A query gives Friends some way to consider the matter deeply. Otherwise, it can be difficult to process a numerical report.

Once a meeting has named its condition—"our institutional structure is no longer supporting our community"—the record keeper can help with the research and discernment phases. Record keepers may know how such shifts have been handled in the community before. They can tell the stories of the meeting. They can talk about the ways in which the community has responded to the presence of God in their midst. They can place the transition in historical context. Most Friends will be primarily focused on the condition of the meeting right here, right now—or possibly experiencing nostalgia for the past, which the human brain tends to oversimplify. The record keeper can research and tell stories. "Here's the minute that was written the day the purchase of this building was approved." Or, "Here's a newsletter article that was published the week the soup kitchen first opened."

Finally, once the group has discerned sense of the meeting, the record keeper can support the meeting in the transition. If the change is big (restructuring the meeting, merger, laying the meeting down, selling a building), then Friends will need some opportunity to record their memories. The act of recording memories is important for future generations but is also an important spiritual and emotional practice for living Friends. A record keeper might be the one to write down the stories, to collect the photographs, to record audio files, or to edit together a video. The format doesn't matter much as long as it's something that will be easy for the group to do.[2] The process of putting it together is much more important than having a polished, professional-level record at the end.

---

2. It might matter a little for archival preservation purposes. See the later chapter on archives.

For Trustees

A TRUSTEE HAS LEGAL responsibility for the rightful use of the assets of a particular organization. The legal responsibility is usually communal. In other words, trustee does not have sole personal responsibility but a collective responsibility with the other trustees. Laws differ by nation and area, but generally speaking, trustees must see that the organization's property is used in the best interest of the organization. If the organization is legally dissolved, the trustees must see that the assets are disposed of properly.

Not all local meetings have trustees. The law may not require them in your area, or your legal status may not require them. Sometimes regions or yearly meetings have trustees instead of the local meeting. Other times, the local meeting and the region and the yearly meeting all have trustees.

The very existence of Quaker trustees may seem odd. In many places, Friends have trustees only because we are legally required to do so. There's tension here because Friends believe that decisions are made by corporate discernment, which means that the body as a whole has ultimate responsibility for the assets of the organization. Absent nonprofit law, we probably wouldn't designate a separate group of Friends to hold this responsibility—although when the trustees have real expertise and do the job well, Friends benefit from the arrangement.

Friends' meetings have dealt with the trustee/corporate discernment disconnect in various ways. Some say that trustees have responsibility in name only, but the trustees are not empowered to make any decisions of any kind without the corporate discernment of the entire body. Others grant trustees total authority to make decisions about the meeting's assets. Most local meetings attempt a middle road: trustees can make certain types of decisions but ask for the discernment of the whole before making others.

For Trustees

The most important thing is that everyone—trustees and meeting members—understands which of these models the meeting is using. Every trustee-related conflict I have ever seen has stemmed from a fundamental disagreement about the role of trustees. These disagreements are not malicious. In fact, they generally aren't even conscious. They exist because the meeting doesn't talk about the role of trustees, so no one knows there is a misunderstanding until that misunderstanding has already produced conflict. There is no "right" Quakerly definition of this relationship, but both the trustees and the other members of the meeting need to know what the local definition is: what kinds of decisions are trustees empowered to make?

Trustees will often be among the first to notice when the institutional structure of the meeting is no longer supporting the community. They will see when the meeting is using its savings to pay routine expenses. They will know if the meeting has an oppressive amount of debt. Trustees may also notice if essential property upkeep isn't getting done.

When this happens, trustees can articulate these observations for the meeting. They might have to tell the story several times before Friends respond. As I've written in other sections, we humans have a remarkable ability to deny change is happening and then, after acknowledging it, to believe it will simply go away. But trustees, because of their unique position, can be specific and honest about the consequences of inaction and can calmly—but repeatedly—raise the issue.

Meetings in the later stages of the life cycle sometimes reach a point of crisis before making institutional adaptations, such as selling a building or restructuring or merging with another meeting or laying the meeting down. This can be especially hard for trustees, who may feel severe pressure because of the particular responsibility they have for good stewardship of the meeting's assets. It's very difficult to stand in front of a group and explain that the meeting will be out of money in five years. Trustees may be tempted to demand action.

But even in emergency situations, the meeting discerns its own future. This is vital both theologically and practically. If the trustees make big decisions without corporate discernment, or if they push too hard for a particular course of action, there will almost inevitably be a backlash in which Friends push against action harder than they otherwise might have. The process of discernment prepares us to accept the results of that discernment. Trustees are very often several steps ahead of the group because they have already spent so much time in discernment among themselves, and they will have to have a lot of patience to participate fully in the meeting's corporate discernment process. Regardless, it's vital that they do, especially because Friends who are coming from another point of view may have insights that the trustees have not considered.

Once the meeting has named its condition—"our institutional structure is no longer supporting our community"—and moved into discernment about next steps, trustees have several supportive roles. They can research alternatives, suggest helpful outside resources, and tell the historical stories of the assets. They can also work hard on transparency, ensuring that everyone understands the available options, including the options that trustees themselves may not think are a good idea.

When the meeting is actually moving through a transition, trustees will probably hire professionals such as lawyers or real estate agents when needed. They can network with Friends from other meetings to get a sense of how those groups have handled similar situations.

If an immediate concern has to do with local law, trustees might ask for help from a local council of churches or interfaith group, since the law applies in the same way to each religious denomination. This is sometimes more practical than consulting with Quaker meetings in a different location where the law itself may not be the same.

One more thing. The nature of trustee work is practical and data oriented. For that reason, trustees tend to write reports to the meeting that are also practical and data oriented. But not all Friends think that way, and some will find it hard to process the information if that's the only manner in which it is presented. It helps if trustees can tell the story four ways: the data story (numbers and trends), the logical progression story (exactly what happens first, second, third), the emotional/historical story (how this fits with our love for each other and our historical context), and the spiritual journey story (explicit acknowledgement of response to God's leadings).

For Regional or Yearly Meeting Clerks or Staff

SOME QUAKER BOOKS OF discipline don't have any indication of who takes responsibility for helping a struggling meeting. Of those that do, most give the responsibility to the region[1]. This works pretty well if the regional meeting is present and functional. Unfortunately, some yearly meetings do not have regions, and some regions struggle to fulfill their own basic functions.

To sum up: some yearly meetings do not have a concrete plan for supporting local meetings; other yearly meetings have a plan, but it's no longer functioning well. Even yearly meetings that have a reasonable, functional plan to support struggling meetings often don't discuss it much for fear of seeming pessimistic, which means that many Friends don't know that help is available.

The end result of this confusion is that regional and yearly meeting clerks and staff often have a responsibility of walking alongside meetings in transition, but they themselves may not be aware of that responsibility—until they find themselves needing to do it. This can be alarming. Friends in such positions may have agreed to serve for entirely different reasons. Then, they suddenly discover they're being asked to invest time and energy and a skill set they may not possess in helping a meeting through a change process.

Regional and yearly meeting clerks and staff—or others with explicit responsibility for walking alongside meetings—can help in a number of

1. Friends do not have consistent terminology for the defined body that is larger than a local meeting and smaller than a yearly meeting. For that reason, I'm using the terms "region" and "regional meeting" to mean quarterly meetings, half-yearly meetings, area meetings, and so forth. Those various terms have slightly different meanings, but the differences are minor enough that the word "region" should work as shorthand.

ways. Not all meetings will need every kind of help, and like any "help," this will only be effective in the context of relationship and faithfulness to Spirit. If God is not guiding us in our work, we have missed something.

Building trust. This step can be taken long before the meeting needs or asks for help, and most meetings will not ask for help in the absence of trust. We build trust by demonstrating reliability and care. A good start might be occasional visits to local meetings, although that's difficult for a staff member that works with many local meetings—in which case phone calls or handwritten notes can make a difference. Even more important is follow-through, which includes responding promptly to all emails or phone calls and demonstrating ways in which the local meeting's actions and reports have influenced the work of the wider organization.

Sometimes, a regional or yearly meeting clerk or staff member will find themselves in a situation of distrust because of something done (or not done) by a Friend who held the same position previously. In this case, deep listening, additional contacts, apology, and possibly restitution can help rebuild the trust relationship.

Normalizing the conversation. Friends sometimes resist considering institutional adaptations, especially big ones, because doing so brings up feelings of guilt or failure or shame. But such conversations can be seeded in the regional and yearly meetings through workshops, newsletters, reports, and interest groups. The more often Friends have heard about other meetings being laid down, or renting out their property, or restructuring into worship groups (and so forth), the more likely it is that Friends will consider such things normal and relatively easy to discuss.

Prayer. Friends who serve a regional or yearly meeting might pray for the local meetings in that organization, perhaps choosing one or two every day. This can also be a time of listening for God's promptings. What is the right way to show love for, or build trust with, the Friends in this particular meeting?

Naming the condition of the meeting. This is a tricky one. It's usually best if someone from the local meeting is the first to name the condition of the meeting—"our institutional structure is no longer supporting our community." But if no one in the local meeting has done so, and if there is a preexisting trusting relationship, a Friend from the region or yearly meeting might be led to take this up. In these cases, it might best be phrased as a query: "Is your institutional structure still supporting your Spirit-led work? Is it possible your structure is demanding too much of your time and energy?"

For Regional or Yearly Meeting Clerks or Staff

Affirming the gifts of Friends in the web. Sometimes we talk about our Quaker structures as if we exist in a set of chains: the local meeting is linked to the regional meeting, the regional meeting is linked to the yearly meeting, and the yearly meeting is linked to the umbrella organization. This can make us think that only Friends serving in a formal, large-group position can walk alongside local meetings.

But actually, Quaker structures aren't meant to be sets of chains. They're more like a web. The regional meeting is an organization with a committee structure and so forth, but more importantly, the regional meeting is composed of all the Friends in all the local meetings within it. And the yearly meeting is composed of all the Friends in all the local and regional meetings within it. We might better understand the relationships like a spider web, in which each local meeting is placed at the intersection of several threads. We can move in any direction along those threads, and one local meeting is connected to every other local meeting in the world, though some are more closely related than others.

Regional and yearly meeting clerks and staff members don't have unlimited time. Nor do they have all the possible spiritual gifts or skill sets. But there may well be Friends in the regional or yearly meeting who do have the necessary time, energy, spiritual gifts, and skill sets to walk alongside meetings in particular ways. Each time we notice and affirm the gifts of an individual Friend, we are making space for the development of those gifts and for the Friend to use those gifts in service.

For example, we might matchmake a local meeting that needs help writing rental agreements for its property with a gifted administrator from another meeting who has been through a similar process. Or we might connect a Friend with experience in grief counseling with a meeting that is working through significant change. Service like this does not need a formal committee appointment. It is ministry.[2]

Providing options. A friend once told me that we rarely experience leadings from God to do something that we have never heard of. It happens, but it's not common. That's because our deep listening to Spirit is always filtered through our past experiences. Therefore, it's important that meetings have a sense of the breadth of options available. It's not a choice between the status quo and laying down the meeting. There are lots of possibilities, many of which are detailed in this book, and a regional or yearly

---

2. Ministry, in the long term, requires its own forms of support, but that is outside the scope of this particular book.

meeting clerk or staff member can introduce these various ideas to a meeting that seems receptive.

Accompaniment for local meeting leadership. A local meeting clerk, trustee, pastor, or ministry and counsel member may commit enormous amounts of time and energy into guiding the meeting through institutional change, and these Friends sometimes grow frustrated or hopeless or angry in the process. They may need a confidant—sometimes for venting, and sometimes for worship and prayer. A regional or yearly meeting staff member or clerk can either provide this directly or suggest that it may be needed.

Gently structuring the step-by-step. We all think differently. For some of us, defining the steps of a process is instinctive. For others, it might be difficult. Some meetings may find that no one in the meeting has the ability to structure the process of discernment and change: what comes first, what comes second, and so forth. If the meeting has asked for help, a regional or yearly meeting staff member or clerk can provide this.

Discernment support. Some meetings may struggle to move through discerning their future. They might find themselves entangled in conflict or reach a certain point and then be unable to affirm sense of the meeting. A regional or yearly meeting staff member or clerk, if invited into the process, can suggest alternative frameworks for consideration, can name a partial sense of the meeting if there seems to be one, or can introduce tools such as facilitated conversations or threshing sessions.

Practical or financial support. Meetings that are changing often discover they need skill sets they've never needed before. For example, a meeting selling property may need a lawyer and a realtor, some form of research into the deed of the meetinghouse, and help with questions about burial grounds. A meeting that is restructuring or merging or laying itself down might need to figure out what will be done with investment funds and endowments. If the regional or yearly meeting isn't able to provide guidance in these areas, the local meeting finds itself moving forward by trial and error when, in fact, there are many other meetings that have already been through such a process.

Other meetings will require financial support in order to move forward. If the meeting is genuinely out of money, which is sometimes the case, it may not be possible to hire a lawyer or make small but necessary pre-sale repairs. In these cases, the regional or yearly meeting staff member or clerk can connect the meeting to potential financial resources. Regional and yearly meetings might even consider creating small funds preemptively that can be used to help a meeting lay itself down or go through some significant transition.

Defining new relationships when the meeting restructures. In most cases, a worship group or preparative meeting does not hold membership, own property, maintain large financial investments, conduct marriages and memorial meetings, or hold legal status as a distinct non-profit organization. Monthly meetings that are nearing the end of their life cycle may need to restructure into one of these simpler forms, but if that happens, the regional or yearly meeting will need to answer a number of questions. Under whose care will the new worship group or preparative meeting be?

Historically, this would be another monthly meeting, though some have suggested experimenting with placing such groups directly under the care of the region. Whatever group holds the smaller body in its care will, at a minimum, take responsibility for its membership records, new members, marriages, and memorial meetings. It will usually also take over its property and financial resources and place the group under its own legal umbrella. Generally, such changes will need the guidance and possibly the approval of the region or the yearly meeting. Someone—most likely the regional or yearly meeting clerk or staff member—will need to anticipate all of the logistical, legal, spiritual, and relational questions involved in such a shift and shepherd the change process in a transparent and reasonably timely way.

Distinct from all of the above is engaging with a "ghost meeting," which is the subject of the next section.

Ghost Meetings

THERE IS ONE MAJOR exception to the general rule of "the meeting discerns its own future." It's what I've come to call "ghost meetings." These are local meetings that exist only in a legal and procedural sense. They may own property. They may have investments. They may even have living members. But everyone, or nearly everyone, has moved away, stopped attending, or died. Worship may not happen, or it may happen occasionally as a special event, composed entirely of visitors. The meeting does not conduct business or take on any of the necessary functions of a meeting, simply because no one is actively participating.

Ghost meetings are the natural result of meetings that don't lay themselves down while they're still able. Among Friends, there is no external organizational force that can say to a still-functioning meeting, "It's time to lay the meeting down." The meeting discerns its own future. But if a meeting waits too long, it becomes a ghost meeting, incapable of doing discernment. This can easily happen by accident rather than neglect. A meeting can go from five worshiping members to none in only a year or two. Members experience major health challenges or family pressures or emergency relocations. During that kind of crisis, the members of the meeting may recognize that something needs to be done, but no one is able to invest time and energy in doing it. Very quickly, the meeting has no active members.

Only the regional or yearly meeting can lay down a ghost meeting, and doing so may not be easy. In fact, some clerks and staff members have deliberately not engaged with ghost meetings because of the time and energy required. When no one acts, the ghost meeting continues to exist, usually silently, on the books. If the ghost meeting has no property, no bank accounts, and no legal obligations, this might not be disastrous. But if the meeting has property, money, or ministries, something needs to be done.

The first step is to define a small group, which I'll call the "core group," to do the spiritual work of discernment. It's obviously not sufficient for one Friend to recognize the presence of a ghost meeting and immediately take steps to close it. The group might be a regional committee or a yearly meeting committee. Or, if there is no obvious, appropriate, and functional regional or yearly meeting group to take on this work, the group can be formed by asking the question, "What is possible and feels appropriate?" This might lead to forming a group that includes spiritually grounded Friends from nearby meetings, a Friend with experience in property management, a clerk or staff member from the regional or yearly meeting, a former member of the meeting or a relative of a former member (even if that person is geographically far away), an archivist or historian, and/or someone who has been through the process of laying down a meeting before.

The core group, once established, may worship together several times, if possible in the ghost meeting's former worship space. The question to hold would be, "Are we called to lay this meeting down?" If the answer to that question is either *yes* or *probably*, the core group will need to begin three distinct but related processes: the procedural Quaker process, the pastoral care process, and the legal process.

From a Quaker point of view, a ghost meeting is not an island. It is probably part of a regional meeting. It is almost certainly part of a yearly meeting. Because we recognize and honor those connections, the ghost meeting can't be laid down without some type of involvement from the larger group. Very few books of discipline have any guidance about how a ghost meeting can be laid down, so chances are good that the procedure will have to be invented.

The first step is to identify the relevant larger group. This is most likely the regional meeting. But if no regional meeting exists, or if the regional meeting is not fully functional, the larger group may be the yearly meeting or even an umbrella organization.

Once the larger group is identified, the core group's steps might be as follows: inform, invite, bring along, and conclude.

To "inform" the larger group is simple but not necessarily easy. This is making sure the larger group knows that the core group is moving toward laying down the meeting. It's important to be clear, at this time, whether this discernment is or is not final. If the group is still open to input from others about alternative possibilities, it should say so. If it is not, that should also be clear, along with an explanation as to why the discernment is final. This informing step can happen in written form or oral form, hopefully both, so that the information will reach as many Friends in the larger group as possible.

In conjunction with this is the second step, "invite," in which the core group makes clear what sorts of contributions are needed or welcome from other Friends. Prayer for the core group? Additional volunteers for the core group? Joining specific discernment gatherings? Stories about the meeting? Financial contributions toward hiring legal assistance? This invitation has three purposes: to solicit help that is needed, to preempt offers of assistance that *aren't* needed, and to give Friends meaningful ways to participate in honoring the life of the meeting.

As the core group engages in the work of laying down the meeting, it will need to "bring along" the Friends in the larger group. Participating in discernment is what prepares us to accept the results of that discernment. So if the core group is working through disposition of assets, for example, or transferring memberships, it's best to find ways to at least report this to the larger group and, if possible, create ways for the larger group to participate in the process. Without this bringing along, it may appear to Friends in the larger group as though the core group simply disappeared for two years and then came back having made decisions in which no one else was consulted. The process should be as transparent and inclusive as possible while still being effective.

Lastly, the core group may "conclude" the work with the larger group in a number of ways, possibly including approval of its final plans. Approval of the larger group is not always required, and the core group can decide whether it's right to ask for such approval. At a minimum, the core group should make a final report, explaining what will happen to the meeting's members (if any) and resources (if any) and historical records. This final step can also include an invitation to the larger group to mark the meeting's ending with a special meeting for worship.

Separately from the technical Quaker procedures, the core group will need to engage in a pastoral care process. This means attending to Friends who have been part of the meeting, Friends who have cared about the meeting although they haven't been part of it, and sometimes also people in the neighborhood.

Ghost Meetings

Sometimes a ghost meeting will still have living members. The core group will need to look at the membership list (sometimes beginning by finding it) and contact each of the meeting's members. Do they wish to maintain their membership in the Religious Society of Friends? If so, do they prefer to transfer their membership to a meeting where they are living now, or do they prefer to have their membership transferred to another meeting nearby the ghost meeting? These conversations are part of the pastoral care work, not only the Quaker procedural work, because the conversations themselves will be spiritual opportunities and possibly emotionally difficult. Contacting members may reveal that some have died. Others may be carrying anger or grief or deep love—or all three—for the meeting community as it used to be.

Aside from membership matters, Friends who have been part of the meeting may need opportunities to ask questions and share their memories. This may include Friends who have never been members of the meeting but whose spouses, parents, or grandparents were. Friends from nearby meetings may also need opportunities to grieve. They may have had close relationships with Friends in the ghost meeting. They may have attended marriages or memorial meetings in the building. Someone needs to provide group and individual opportunities for such Friends to share their stories. Archiving these stories can also be helpful, whether in written or audio or video form. The process of preserving stories is useful for future historians and also meaningful to Friends in the present.

The final group that may need pastoral care is the neighbors. In some cases, this isn't a concern at all. But in other cases, there might be attachments to the meeting or the property that aren't obvious. Neighborhood children might be accustomed to playing in the yard. Older people may have benefitted from, or participated in, neighborhood ministries that closed a generation ago. A family might remember receiving a basket of baked goods from the meeting's pastor as a welcome when they first moved into the neighborhood. By learning about and acknowledging these relationships—either by knocking on doors or by holding a public gathering of some sort—the core group can invite the neighbors to say goodbye in a meaningful way rather than wonder what happened to the meeting and why.

Finally, Friends in the core group will need to move through a number of practical and logistical matters, including making decisions about the ghost meeting's property and its investments. While more information about these practical matters can be found in other sections of this book, it's most important to remember that ideally, the property and investments will be given to causes that were historically important to the meeting. For example, a meeting may have had ministries to the homeless throughout its life, or perhaps the meeting had a particularly strong program for neighborhood children twenty years ago. These are signals about how God has worked through this meeting in the past. The meeting's legacy can be honored by allowing such historical ministries to guide the core group's discernment about dispensation of assets, although it's important to check first that the meeting's establishing documents and donor-directed funds do not require the assets to be distributed in some other manner.

For Traveling Ministers

THE TRADITION OF TRAVELING ministers goes back to the earliest days of Friends, and we still have these ministers. Not all traveling ministers fill the same functions or even similar ones. Their work varies in topic, in medium, and in structure. For the purposes of this section, I'm defining "traveling minister" as expansively as possible—a Friend who visits various Friends' meetings over a period of time under divine leading.

The traveling minister, who is a stranger to the local meeting, may have freedom that others do not. The stranger can often say things—and be heard—that members of the community itself either cannot say or cannot say in a way that the message will be received. A traveling minister's words may seem less threatening because they can so easily be ignored. After all, the meeting might not even see this Friend again. Also, Friends usually aren't aware of the traveling minister's own human flaws, especially if the visit is short, so whatever is said won't be rejected out of hand because of complicated relationships or history.

Most Friends in most local meetings don't often visit other faith communities. For this reason, Friends in a local meeting often don't have much perspective about the condition of the meeting itself. It is the only one they know. They may be able to compare its current condition to what they remember of its history, or compare its current condition to what they wish it were, or compare its current condition to one or two other meetings they've known. But they are unlikely to have a breadth of experiences with local faith communities.

The traveling minister probably does have a breadth of experiences and therefore a perspective that Friends in the local meeting don't have.

This perspective is important because the traveling minister can name for the local meeting the gifts of that local meeting.

The gifts of local meetings are hugely variable. One might approach things with laughter and good humor. Another might have a unique love for children. Yet another might treat its employees extremely well. Understanding these strengths *as* strengths not only gives Friends a sense of hope about their local meeting. It also provides some food for thought about what is special and should not be lost.

A traveling minister may also perceive the local meeting's weaknesses, including but not limited to institutional structures that aren't working. Sometimes it is right to name these. Other times, that naming will only cause hurt. If the naming is called for, it might come as part of a message in worship or simply as a curious question over a cup of tea. Usually, what's needed is a gentle and invitational tone—but of course, any traveling minister should rely primarily on Spirit's guidance regarding what to say and what not to say.

There are several ways that a traveling minister can help a meeting that is already in transition. One is simple affirmation. "This is a really difficult thing." Or, "I see how faithfully you're working." When Friends are tired, engaged in conflict, or mired in logistics, affirmation can be a balm. When I am traveling among Friends, I sometimes phrase this affirmation as an expression of thanks. "I am so grateful for the love and dedication you're showing to your community. It's really beautiful, and I know how much it matters in the long run. Thank you for your service."

The traveling minister can also hold the meeting in prayer, with or without telling Friends they are doing so.

A traveling minister can suggest relevant written resources to meetings in transition, such as books or articles or websites. It can be important to listen first and offer resources only later, since depending on what phase of transition the meeting is in, an influx of information can be more of a distraction than it is helpful. Sometimes the traveling minister will also know of another meeting that has been through a very similar process. It can be comforting for Friends to know they are not alone, regardless of whether or how much they reach out to another group for assistance.

If it's appropriate, a traveling minister might offer to be in ongoing relationship with a local meeting in transition. But it's important to recognize the boundaries of one's own gifts and leadings. Meetings in transition need a variety of things at a variety of times—discernment support, research, grief work, practical alternatives, facilitated discussions, and so forth. If what the meeting most needs is not in keeping with what the minister is called to or equipped to do, it might be better to offer prayer (and perhaps the name of someone else whose work is more in keeping with the need).

The other piece that traveling ministers must remember is respect for preexisting and ongoing relationships. Nearly all local meetings are connected to regional meetings, yearly meetings, and/or umbrella organizations, and some of these larger groups have staff or committees or procedures specifically designed to help meetings through transitions. To be in right relationship with the local meeting means to also be in right relationship with the larger group, being sure that the traveling minister's work is not interfering with long-term relationships or worsening a conflict between the local meeting and the larger community.

Conflict

IN THE CONTEXT OF a Quaker meeting, conflict usually happens because two or more people have different ideas about what should be done. Sometimes their goals are different. Other times, the goals are the same, but there's a disagreement about the best way to reach them. We usually only name something as "conflict" if it's not immediately possible to take on both ideas at the same time.

In a very basic sense, conflict almost always exists at the beginning of a discernment process, though it's often conflict without bad feelings. This is because corporate discernment starts with a question. If the correct answer to the question was uniformly obvious, we probably wouldn't ask it.

In many cases, conflict within corporate discernment becomes a powerful generative force. One person speaks. That message settles over the group. Another person speaks. A different perspective makes us all step back and consider the situation differently. A third person speaks. We see a way in which the first two ideas might complement each other. A fourth person speaks. The compilation of perspectives brings a crack of Light we would never have noticed before...

In corporate discernment, we rely on God's assistance to listen deeply. We can do this at other times, too, in conflicts that rise about where to put the table for coffee hour or which child claimed the bicycle first. Whether a conflict is large or small, long-term or short-term, we can try to engage with it as a generative force.

Unfortunately, conflict can also be a powerful destructive force. Sometimes we never find a solution that can adequately meet the goals of each person. Other times, we're never able to try. Sometimes one or more Friends aren't willing to consider alternatives. Other times, one or more Friends don't trust the intentions of the "other side"—and that mistrust may or may not be justified. On still other occasions, we're not able to work through conflict because what is framed as conflict is actually abuse or one individual's harmful behavior patterns. These situations need to be handled much differently, so when we approach them as conflict, we will not resolve them.

There are people who thrive on conflict, but among Quakers, it seems like the majority is conflict-avoidant. Unfortunately, avoiding conflict—while it's sometimes more comfortable in the short term—almost never prevents a conflict from becoming destructive. There are many books written about how to approach conflict, but the single practice I've found most helpful is bravely asking for a conversation.

As many Christians do, Friends draw from the Gospel of Matthew for guidance in addressing conflict. First, speak directly to the other person. If that doesn't work, ask for help from a small group or another individual, like a clearness committee or a pastor or a conflict transformation group. If resolution still can't be found, bring the issue to the whole meeting.

For that first meeting, if a one-on-one conversation feels too hard, one or both Friends might invite an elder to be present. The elder does not need a formal title in the meeting; what I mean here is the old sense of the Quaker term "elder," which described Friends of any age who were spiritually grounded, wise, and gifted in accompaniment. When elders are present in this context, they usually say very little and mostly ground the encounter in prayer.

The steps derived from Matthew are relevant if a situation involves two or more people in an actual conflict, but it is never reasonable or Spirit-led to expect a victim to sit down one-on-one with an abuser. When the so-called "conflict" is actually abuse, harassment, bullying, or other forms of destructive behavior from an individual, it becomes a matter of concern for the community's integrity. Most often, a pastor or ministry and counsel committee needs to intervene and set clear, reasonable boundaries on the person's behavior. Setting boundaries does not mean we don't love the person behaving destructively. It means that we do love this person, and they deserve to hear the truth and receive firm, clear expectations. It also means that the community and the individuals in it deserve protection from serious harm.

One final note: in cases of destructive behavior, if that behavior has risen to the point of breaking the law—especially laws about abuse—we should call law enforcement. Not doing so sets off a chain reaction that almost always allows harm to happen again.

Why is all this included in a book about institutional transitions? Because so many transitions happen in the shadow of old conflict. Often, though not always, something happened in the meeting years before that was never resolved and continues to shape our relationships with each other and the meeting. We are still avoiding it, or still experiencing the pain of it, or still blaming someone else for it. Even Friends who arrived after the conflict and know nothing about it probably feel its impact.

The old conflict may have nothing to do with the meeting's current condition. Other times, it's directly related, having been part of what moved the meeting from one stage of its life cycle to another. Either way, if a meeting is trying to go through institutional adaptation, chances are good that it will trip over the old conflict. Friends who were hurt, or who are still angry, may find themselves expressing those emotions in conversations that are theoretically unrelated. If the meeting has never been through stages of truth-telling, repentance, restitution, and forgiveness, it might not be possible to make significant change. In this kind of situation, so much energy goes into suppressing the old conflict and working around it that no energy is left to do more than preserve the status quo.

Sometimes the old conflict can still be worked through. If many of the Friends who were involved are still present, they can each have the opportunity to explain how they remember the situation and how they feel about what happened now. When exploring old conflict, our memories may differ significantly from one another's. What's most important is deep listening and the willingness to believe that the other person's memory may be at least partially accurate. . .and that they are speaking in good faith about what they actually recall. I might say that I do not remember doing what someone else says I did but, at the same time, name that it's possible I did it and I do not remember—and if that is the case, I sincerely apologize and give my word not to repeat those actions. If the person I wronged is no longer in the community and is not accessible, I can express these same feelings to God in a repentance process. Similarly, I (or we, the meeting as a whole) can make restitution when this is possible. We can also practice forgiveness when that's what's needed—individual forgiveness or forgiveness of or for an entire group.

There are times when old conflict can't be worked through at all, most especially conflict that is a generation or more old but is still impacting

Conflict

the meeting. In these cases, the best we can do is acknowledge the conflict—share what we know and what we've been told and what we think we remember. Again, this must be done with care and deep mutual listening and the guidance of Spirit. We can grieve an old conflict by telling its story and honoring its impact, even if it's no longer possible to resolve it.

An old conflict is often part of a meeting's story. Once we have acknowledged it, worked through it, and/or had an opportunity to grieve it, it becomes an integrated part of who we are. It becomes part of our story of how our community has responded to the presence of God in our midst—because sometimes, the way we respond is "poorly." Both we and the generations after us can learn from our mistakes. When we are preserving the history of the meeting, even in archives, the most desperately hurtful times are every bit as much a part of the history as the most memorable celebrations.

Changing the Committee Structure

"Our institutional structure is no longer supporting our community." The first time a meeting encounters this problem, it's almost always because the committee structure is too big. Of course, it didn't start out that way. When the meeting was larger, it was necessary to develop eight or twelve or fifteen committees. We were called to a lot of work, and many Friends wanted to serve. Over time, our numbers grew smaller. At first, we had a little trouble filling the slots. Then considerable trouble. We reduced the number of positions on each committee from eight Friends to five. But a few years later, we still couldn't fill them all, and it didn't feel right to just eliminate committees. After all, they wouldn't exist if there weren't important work to do.

A meeting in this position may need to change its entire committee structure. This will most likely become clear when a significant role (such as clerk or treasurer) can't be filled or when there's a sudden avalanche of Friends leaving committees, feeling overworked and spiritually exhausted. The meeting has reached a point at which the community is supporting the institutional structure, rather than the other way around.

In the section called "Why Adapting is Hard," I pointed out a number of reasons why Friends resist change. One is worth rearticulating here, which is confusion between a concern and a leading. The meeting may resist laying down committees because it's obvious that each has important work. But a deep spiritual knowing that something must be done is a *concern*. Friends take up work when they have a *leading*—that is, a specific spiritual prompting that God is asking *me* or *us* to do *this* thing *now*. If no one is able or willing to do the work, it's probably not a leading. . .or if we're sure it's a leading, but we can't get it done, then we need to change something else to make space for it.

Committee structures, as they exist in most Quaker meetings, tend to favor certain types of spiritual gifts and specific kinds of leadings. People with strong organizational and writing gifts may thrive in committee settings. But the work of such Friends is not more important than the work of a Friend with spiritual accompaniment gifts who is led to serve food at coffee hour and provide comforting conversation in the kitchen. Nor the work of a Friend with leadership gifts who is led to coordinate an ecumenical drop-in center for the cold and hungry. But the nature of a committee structure is to formalize, and thus make seem important, the first type of service and not the others.

Of all the ways in which we might organize service, committees are the most rigid approach available. They have specific job descriptions. Their membership is tightly controlled and documented. Friends on committees must ask for permission or approval from the meeting to do anything unusual. There is no space, within a defined committee structure, for a Friend to follow a leading that does not align with that committee structure. Nor can a Friend agree to do part of a committee's charge and not another part, not even if that Friend is literally unable to take on the entire assignment.

We can structure our service to the meeting in several other ways: with a focus on tasks rather than roles, with the use of working groups and task groups and volunteers, and with affirmation of ministries.

Focus on tasks rather than roles. A formal committee structure convinces us that we have roles to fill. Actually, we have tasks to be done. Even if a meeting's property committee has been responsible for mowing the lawn and tidying the bulletin boards for the last thirty-five years, there is no compelling spiritual reason why the same group must mow the lawn as tidies the bulletin boards. If we are having trouble filling the property committee, we might try making a list of all the tasks the property committee has been doing. Soon enough, one Friend may volunteer to mow the lawn while another Friend volunteers to tidy bulletin boards. Neither had the necessary time or energy to join the property committee (and attend regular meetings and fix the furnace and hire a roof repairperson and plant flowers), but this way, at least some of the work will get done—and the property committee has two things off its plate.

Even very central roles, like that of a clerk, can be divided into tasks. Perhaps one Friend prepares agendas and sends emails while another clerks the business meeting. If a treasurer can't be found, maybe one Friend will serve as a bookkeeper while another deposits checks and a third writes reports. Focusing on tasks is not a cure-all, but it does allow Friends to take on responsibilities that align with their gifts and that don't feel overwhelming.

Working groups, task groups, and volunteers. Friends have no common, universal definition of these terms, but I'm going to define them here in order to illustrate the various approaches available to us. Generally speaking, Friends can use whatever terms they like, as long as everyone present understands what's meant.

A committee, as I've said, has a formal, written charge and some kind of appointment process. They are often helpful for routine tasks, especially the types of tasks that require institutional memory. A committee is likely to have minutes and other internal resources. It's also likely to have overlap in terms of service, so that more experienced members of the committee can train less experienced members. Committees, because of their formal structures, can easily perpetuate work that must be done again and again—but those same formal structures make them hard to lay down.

A working group may or may not have a formal, written charge. It usually comes together around a concern rather than a specific task—for example, a concern for a discipleship class in the meeting, or a concern for seeding native plants in the meetinghouse garden. It's composed of volunteers who are led to take on the concern together. The working group can decide when it is ready to be laid down. Working groups are perfect for situations that require flexibility, especially when we're not exactly sure what tasks need to be done. But the lack of formal structure can sometimes lead to mission drift.

A task group is temporary. It is formed—as the name suggests—to complete a specific task. It generally has a specific but short-term charge, often developed spontaneously in the context of a business meeting. "Judy and Roberto are asked to research whether it's practical to install a compost toilet in the meetinghouse" is an example of a minute that forms a task group. Judy and Roberto will then do the research, and the task group is automatically laid down after they report back. Task groups are well suited for important jobs that only need to be done once, and they tend to be easier to fill than a long-term committee. Sometimes, they will lead to the formation of another type of group, such as a working group to oversee the process of installing a compost toilet—but Judy and Roberto are under no obligation to join that working group once their original task is done,

Changing the Committee Structure

which means they can commit to one piece of work without fear that they'll wind up doing much more.

Volunteer roles are a good match for things that just need doing. Perhaps we always need a Friend to do dishes after coffee hour, or to serve as a greeter, or to help in the meetinghouse library. The most expedient way of making that happen is a well-publicized sign-up sheet. We don't need to worry about the skill set of the volunteers, because it's unlikely that anyone will do the dishes so badly as to cause permanent damage. And the accessibility of simple volunteer roles provides newcomers with an easy way to engage with the community.

Affirmation of ministry. Some Friends experience a call to particular work in the community. Pastoral groups recognize this in the form of Quaker pastors. Some non-pastoral groups record ministers, and most of us remember that historically, Friends recorded ministers and elders and what we called overseers. Roughly speaking, these were terms for preachers, spiritual caregivers, and practical caregivers.

Friends still experience calls to ministry, and these come in many forms. A Friend might be called to a ministry of baking, or speaking, or writing, or protesting, or advocating for children's rights, or hospital visits, or teaching. A ministry is led by Spirit, is aligned with the gifts that God has given the minister, and tends to persist for some time.

We can affirm ministry by helping Friends with the initial discernment process (sometimes but not always by using a clearness committee). If Friends are clear that there is a legitimate call to ministry, we can support and nurture that ministry by allowing it to be practiced, providing a channel of accountability, and—if necessary—offering financial or logistical support. A ministry differs from service on a committee because it is a response to a calling, not an agreement to take on a pre-designated list of tasks. It may also be focused internally (in service to the local meeting community) or externally (in service to the neighborhood, the Religious Society of Friends, or some other group in the world). We may not be able to count on calls to ministry covering necessary tasks like repairs to the plumbing, but the practice of affirming ministry does allow us to respond specifically to God's unexpected callings in Friends' lives.

How do we actually make the shift from our current committee structure (whatever that may be) to a new way of getting things done?

Some meetings are able to do this fairly simply. Friends gather in a room, talk through the existing committees, and decide to lay some down while converting others into task groups or volunteer roles. There's no need to overcomplicate the process if it seems fairly clear to everyone involved what needs to happen.

In other cases, the situation feels more difficult. Friends disagree about what work needs to be done, or some may resist the idea of making any changes. "If we just all do a little more, it'll be fine." Other times, the group is so large that it's not possible for everyone to agree quickly about next steps. In these cases, we might try a different approach.

See if Friends generally agree there's a problem. In this step, it's not necessary for everyone to agree on what the problem is, simply that a problem exists—in some way, the committee structure isn't functioning adequately. There may be lots of different opinions about the source of the problem or the best possible solution, and that's fine. It's enough to have an informal sense of unity that the current situation isn't working.

Try one or two short-term, non-traditional, not-too-threatening experiments. What would happen if the peace committee took a six-month break from regular meetings? Suppose social hour was done by volunteers for a year while we suspended the formal hospitality committee? Can ministry and counsel try dividing into three topic-specific working groups for a few months? Rather than sending the question about gardeners to the property committee, can we charge two Friends as a task group to do some research?

The purpose of this step is not to find the perfect solution. The purpose of this step is to see how imperfect solutions might feel. Experiments such as these generally don't require approval from everyone in the meeting, and they're a way to find out what works and doesn't work about different approaches. When we experiment, we may decide that the new way is right for now and make it more permanent. Other times, we'll discover that the first idea doesn't work and we should try something else. A habit of experimentation is healthy. There's no such thing as the perfect committee structure for an ever-changing community.

Resist the urge to form a subgroup that will study the problem. Friends often start a change process by creating a new group. The group proceeds to send out surveys, make phone calls, research alternatives, and come back to the meeting a year later with a finalized proposal—which usually will not be accepted. This is because the subgroup has been through a discernment process that everyone else missed, and the act of corporate discernment *is, in itself,* what prepares us to accept the results of that discernment. The rest of the meeting did not experience the conversations that the subgroup

Changing the Committee Structure

experienced. They did not take part in the same spiritual journey. So when they are presented with the results, they are not in a place to accept them.

Smaller steps, especially experiments, are an easier way to collectively try new things, see how they feel, and move in the direction of what the group finds workable. Striving for the perfect system almost always prevents us from progressing. "Perfect" doesn't exist, and it's too easy to reject any plan that isn't perfect. The goal is "more doable than what we have now."

Staff Transitions

MANY MEETINGS WILL MAKE staff transitions as part of an institutional adaptation. If we're running out of money, for example, we may have no choice but to stop having a full-time employee. On the other hand, if we have an abundance of money but a scarcity of energy, we might consider hiring additional staff.

Some meetings will name the condition of the meeting—"our institutional structure is no longer supporting our community"—and will conclude that, if only the right staff members could be found, the situation would improve. Such meetings may think that more or different staff could rejuvenate the meeting and cause it to grow. Then, no other structural changes would be needed.

As I've said previously, a meeting in the second half of its life cycle can certainly grow, but only if the meeting is genuinely led to grow. Growth implies change. It also requires an investment of time and energy. If Friends in the meeting are not genuinely led to change, they will resist change (consciously or unconsciously), and the meeting will not grow—at least, not much—no matter how hard the staff members are working to make it happen. It is unfair and ineffective to blame a meeting's condition on the staff, and doing so tends to launch a cycle of repeated hiring and firing.

That said, sometimes staff adjustments are precisely what is needed, especially in financial shortfall. If a meeting is moving from a full-time staff member to a part-time staff member, or from two staff members to one staff member, it may help to focus on tasks and gifts rather than on roles. Suppose that a meeting's full-time employee has previously been bringing a prepared message twice a month, administrating building rentals, and visiting Friends in the hospital. The meeting has decided that this full-time employee will now be a half-time employee. To which aspects of the job does the employee feel most authentically called? Is this Friend primarily a preacher, primarily an administrator, or primarily a spiritual accompanier? This will give us guidance in which aspects of the job description should be kept.

The meeting can ask itself similar questions. If the staff member will be moving to half-time work and the meeting is not making other adjustments, then someone will still need to preach, to do building administration, and to make visits. Are there Friends in the meeting who carry prophetic gifts and who are able to bring messages? Are there Friends in the meeting who carry gifts of administration and who are willing to answer emails and coordinate rentals? Are there Friends in the meeting who carry accompaniment gifts and who are prepared to make hospital visits? The answers to these questions will give us guidance in which aspects of the staff job description to cut—because other members of the community are able to take on those responsibilities.

There is no correct set of tasks for the half-time employee. By adapting the job description according to the gifts and leadings of both the staff member and the other Friends in the meeting, we'll be more likely to reach a long-term, workable solution.

A similar process may be useful if the meeting is hiring additional staff. What are all the tasks that require attention in the meeting? Which of these are we already able and led to do? Which of these need more attention than we're able to give? Once those tasks are identified, the right employee can be found. Hiring someone to teach Sunday school is quite different from hiring someone to take minutes and archive records, but neither is unreasonable, depending on the circumstances of the meeting.

Managing employees is difficult, particularly so for a group that is not accustomed to doing it, and especially if the employee will be under supervision of a whole committee. We must remember that, in Friends' understanding, a staff member is a released minister. They are part of our community and neither more nor less important than any other member.

What does it mean to treat our Friend justly? Are we clear in our expectations and how many hours per week we expect the responsibilities to take? Is the payment we offer fair in exchange for the number of hours in the place where we live? If the staff member is confused, or ill, or overburdened, do we have a plan to help our Friend? Are we prepared to give our Friend freedom to do what we have asked them to do in the manner that works for them? Who is allowed to criticize our Friend's work or offer suggestions, and in what way? When is our Friend "on duty," and when is our Friend given a break for a personal life and spiritual rest?

Any time we make a staff transition, we should ask staff members to track the number of hours worked for a while. As a matter of integrity, half-time pay should be given for half-time hours, and full-time pay for full-time hours, and so forth. If the staff member is not tracking and reporting hours spent, we may never realize that our expectations for a half-time employee, for example, are not appropriate and need to be adjusted.

We'll make mistakes in staff transitions, just as we'll make mistakes in any other type of transition. It's essential that we check in periodically with everyone involved. Is the arrangement still working? Are there changes that would make things better? We can take care to make sure that whoever is working directly with our released ministers is approachable and dependable, so that employees feel genuinely able to express concerns and ask for help.

Hybrid and Online Meetings

As recently as the year 2015, the idea of a hybrid or online Quaker meeting was unimaginable to most Friends. But since that time, both the available technology and our circumstances have changed. Many meetings are now worshiping in a hybrid or online format—"hybrid" meaning that some attend on the internet while others attend physically in the meeting place at the same time, and these two groups can interact in at least some superficial way.

Some meetings accidentally transitioned to being hybrid meetings during the Covid-19 pandemic and then discovered that returning to an in-person-only format did not seem appropriate. That has been difficult for some Friends and a Godsend for others. In some meetings, the question of hybrid-or-not-hybrid has been a source of considerable conflict.

But on the whole, becoming a hybrid or online meeting is no longer unthinkable. In fact, we are quickly coming to view this new condition as normal. In certain cases, becoming an online-only meeting might even be desirable. Shifting to an online-only format can allow a meeting to release its property. Online-only meetings require smaller budgets and can make the meeting accessible to distant or homebound members. This might be especially relevant to a meeting with a large proportion of aging Friends or young, highly mobile members.

But moving to a hybrid or online model impacts the community in ways beyond worship. A meeting that gathers partially or entirely online is no longer a geographic community by nature. It is not more difficult to join an online meeting from far away than it is from nearby, and very soon, the terms "far away" and "nearby" become less relevant. An online community must consider how all of its participants, regardless of physical location, can serve the meeting community, give and receive pastoral care, and participate in social time with the group. Most practices are adaptable, but when a meeting becomes an online community, it's important to realize that meeting life will not be exactly the same as before. Committee descriptions may need to be reconsidered so as to allow meaningful participation by remote members. Pastoral care will change, too; it may not be possible to deliver a meal and have a visit, so a gift card and a phone call might become the new norm. Social time online might need to be more structured, with breakout groups or turn-taking, to ensure that everyone has the opportunity to participate.

An online meeting also begins to lose its specific attachment to the meetinghouse's neighborhood. The building might still be in use (if the meeting is hybrid) or perhaps not usually (if the meeting is online). We may have to consider whether keeping the property is rightly led—for us, and for the physical neighbors of the property who might be affected by the building's lack of use. We may also find ourselves struggling to maintain neighborhood ministries if an increasing proportion of members is geographically distant or not coming to the meetinghouse regularly. These patterns will call us to additional discernment. What is the faithful next step for this meeting now?

Finally, a hybrid or online meeting will need a different approach to inviting and welcoming newcomers. A sign may no longer be relevant, but a strong website will be. Someone will need to pay active attention to who joins worship as a visitor, because there will be no online equivalent of a guestbook at the door. Friends will need structured opportunities to meet newcomers and get to know each other, because the small-group conversations that happen naturally in the social hall are trickier to initiate online.

Any meeting that transitions for any reason from in-person only to hybrid or online will have need to reassess its practices. This is another opportunity to return to our "why"—the Spirit-led purposes behind our traditions—so that we can preserve what we are called to do even as we adjust how we do it.

Combining or Merging Meetings

THERE ARE SEVERAL REASONS why two or more meetings might consider merging. Perhaps both meetings are looking for ways to release more energy for ministry, and they recognize that having only one clerk and one committee structure would make that easier. Perhaps one or both meetings are in a financial shortfall. Perhaps the demographics of the town or city have shifted and the area no longer needs multiple Quaker meetings. Or perhaps one meeting is very small and struggling while the other is comparatively large, which would lead to a different type of merging.

There are several ways in which two or more meetings could come together and combine, depending on the circumstances of each meeting and the results of the meetings' collective discernment.

Approach #1: If one meeting is large and the other much smaller, the smaller meeting may simply come under the care of the other, probably as a worship group. A monthly meeting that is restructuring as a worship group needs to come under the care of another group because worship groups do not hold membership or do business. In these cases, the assets of the worship group would be transferred to the monthly meeting, including both property and investments. The monthly meeting would hold the memberships of Friends in the worship group and be responsible for arranging marriages and memorial meetings as needed. The groups would continue to worship separately but would do business together. All Friends would have an equal responsibility for serving the meeting as a whole, and Friends attending the worship group would be just as likely to hold committee service or other roles as Friends attending the monthly meeting. Lastly, individual Friends attending the monthly meeting would have a responsibility to visit the worship group occasionally, as this is part of the spiritual practice of having a worship group under the meeting's care.

If the meetings are of roughly equal size and vitality, or if an under-the-care relationship does not feel right, then the meetings will likely merge directly into a single unit. But even in this case, there are several potential approaches.

Approach #2: Two or more meetings each become preparative meetings under a new, unified monthly meeting, but they continue to have separate worship, separate facilities, and separate legal identity.

A preparative meeting does not hold membership or conduct monthly meetings, and it may or may not have legal status and property. Many Friends think of the term "preparative" as meaning that the group is preparing to become a monthly meeting. This is historically accurate. But "preparative" can also refer to the meeting preparing business for the monthly meeting, which these groups do. In Approach #2, monthly meetings for business would probably be held at each meetinghouse in turn, with Friends from all preparative meetings attending all of them.

The primary benefit to a limited merger such as this one is simplifying the committee structures of the preparative meetings. They probably would not all need a clerk, a recording clerk, and a full slate of committees. Some would be shared. But because the meetings would each continue to maintain separate property and legal status, this would not solve financial shortfall problems or situations in which property maintenance has become daunting. This model may be most helpful for meetings that need to simplify their procedures somewhat but are geographically too distant for the merged community to gather every week.

Approach #3: Two or more meetings become preparative meetings under a new, unified monthly meeting. They continue to have separate worship, but they share facilities and a legal identity. This arrangement might work best for meetings that have different worship styles. The meetings combine legally (including all assets) and share a building. The groups come together for monthly business meeting but may have partially separate committee structures, and they worship separately, either in different rooms or at different times.

In this scenario, Friends' memberships are all in the same monthly meeting, and the two preparative meetings might start to blend together over time as Friends join one another's worship and work together on committees and ministries. There will probably continue to be some feeling of separate-ness between the meetings for at least a generation, since their worship is separate and the Friends' remembered history is different, but the group only needs one set of significant service roles (treasurer, clerk, etc.) and has only one facility to care for. Friends using this approach might need to be especially careful about balanced committee representation so that one group doesn't have disproportionate power over resource-related decisions.

Approach #4: Two or more meetings combine to become a single monthly meeting. They worship together and share property and a legal identity as a single unit. This is what most Friends imagine when they hear the concept of merging, though as I've just explained, it's not the only available model. In this case, the previously separate meetings are attempting to combine seamlessly, so that which group a Friend "comes from" is mostly irrelevant by the end of the process. It allows the meeting to grow in numbers and function as a much larger community.

Not every merger is successful. In fact, research from the ecumenical world tells us that the majority of mergers result in smaller, not larger, worship communities after the first few years because so many of those involved are dissatisfied and leave.[1] There are specific steps meetings can take, though, that increase the likelihood of a positive merger.

Say the idea out loud. Someone has to be brave enough to make the initial suggestion, which will likely be met by a wide variety of reactions, possibly including incredulity, anger, dismissal, wariness, curiosity, and excitement.

Assume it's possible. A merger is a big step. Friends might be tempted to say, "That would never happen." And perhaps it won't happen. However, assuming something isn't possible is among the least helpful approaches to discernment.

To say "God makes all things possible" is an oversimplification. God makes many things possible, but we generally have to cooperate with God if it's going to work out. A first step toward that cooperation is to assume that a merger could happen, if Friends discerned that it should.

Commit to Spirit-led discernment. A merger might be a faithful next step for the meetings involved. It also might not. We discover this through corporate discernment, which means speaking as led, listening deeply to each other, and finding and affirming sense of the meeting—all of which requires that we trust the community's discernment over our own. Those

---

1. Elliott, *Vital Merger.*

who participate in the discernment process must understand the concept of Spirit-led corporate discernment and commit to it.

Talk about the conditions of the meetings. This can be done formally or informally, but Friends need to get a basic idea of the conditions of each of the meetings, including their own. How many people attend worship regularly? Has that number changed much in recent years? Are there families with children in the meetings? A high proportion of aging Friends? Do the meetings have neighborhood or world ministries? What is the status of the property? Are the meetings in financial shortfall? How are the meetings approaching committees and other forms of service to the meeting? How are Friends feeling about the spiritual condition of their communities?

Worship and pray, together and as separate meetings. It can help to designate a specific period of time, possibly a year, in which the meetings will get to know one another more deeply before attempting specific discernment about a merger. One way to do this is by worshiping and praying together. The meetings might join together for collective worship once a month, or they might arrange a mutual visitation program in which every individual Friend worships with the "other" meeting at least once every six weeks. Friends might also commit to be present for worship with their own meetings as often as possible. Regular worship is part of the preparation for complicated discernment processes.

Have some community-building activities together. Worship is part of building a relationship between two or more communities, but it's not generally sufficient. Community-building activities can also help. These can be playful (board games, movie nights) or social (potlucks, book clubs) or practical (cleaning days, service projects). In fact, because different people tend to build trust in different ways, it's probably best to have multiple types of community-building activities.

Let distant and less-active community members know what's being considered. More people love a meeting than are immediately obvious. Distant members, Friends who grew up in the meeting, and others with connections to the history may not realize that the meeting is considering a merger unless some special effort is made to advise them. As I've said in other places, if these Friends are not given an opportunity to contribute to the meeting's discernment and process the proposal over time, they are likely to appear at the last minute and disrupt whatever progress has been made simply because they have not had the chance to join the spiritual journey of the group.

Combining or Merging Meetings

Give regional and yearly meetings a heads up. In some cases, the regional or yearly meeting will have helpful resources—sometimes practical assistance, sometimes spiritual accompaniment, and sometimes financial support. But even if that is not the case, the wider community needs the opportunity to know that a merger is being explored so that they can pray for the groups involved and are not surprised by a merger at the end of the discernment process.

Hold threshing sessions, for both concerns and joys. Threshing sessions are useful opportunities for Friends to express emotions, articulate fears, and consider new possibilities. They are usually structured as open worship, in which any Friend can speak, but the intention is only to listen deeply to one another. Back-and-forth conversation is not allowed, and no decision is anticipated. Sometimes threshing sessions are guided by queries. Even if there are no queries, a clerk or other facilitator can start the threshing session by explicitly welcoming both expressions of concern and expressions of joy. It can be easy for a threshing session to focus only on what might be difficult, but the community is helped if the threshing session also includes space for what exciting possibilities might unfold.

Develop a shared vision of the new meeting. Friends might be tempted to skip this step. Most of us don't have a mission statement or defined purpose for our meetings, beyond existence as a Quaker meeting, and trying to produce a mission statement often provokes conflict. But a shared vision doesn't have to be restrictive. It might be something as simple as, "We will be a meeting with a small but thriving children's program, shared meals every month, and a worship space that is sunny and welcoming." Naming the shared vision gives us something to work toward. It can also remind us of what's important when the practical steps become difficult.

Begin to draft a document: new name for the merged meeting, what happens to property, staff questions, and so forth. Once Friends have been through the getting-to-know-each-other period and the threshing sessions and have found a shared vision, it's time to consider the practical and legal steps. Most likely, these have already been discussed conceptually, but probably not yet in detail.

Someone (trustees, clerks, a specially appointed working group, or some other body) will need to start putting proposed details in writing. This document won't be the legal document for the merger, but it will be the document that Friends will eventually approve (or not).

Friends might consider a new name for the new meeting, rather than taking one monthly meeting's name or the other. The new name might be representative of the shared vision, or something about the process of merging, or the full geographic area that will be covered. A new name, chosen together, helps the meeting feel like an entirely new entity rather than two or more groups held together by glue.

Often, a merger will involve a change from multiple worship spaces to a single worship space. Rather than assume the communities will move into one building or another, it's worth asking: what is the best property arrangement for our new community? Are we led to own a building? Rent a space? Build a new building? Or something else? It's important that these decisions are practical and also in keeping with the shared vision for the new meeting. For example, if Friends envision a thriving children's program, that implies a need for a dedicated children's space.

When merging, Friends should seriously consider using neither of the former worship spaces. A new worship space, like a new name, can provide a sense of identity to the newly combined meeting. It also prevents anyone from feeling as though they're on the "home team" or the "visitors' team."

If the merging meetings have staff, they may discover they have more staff than they need or can reasonably support—or perhaps they'll discover they have the right number of staff members but with overlapping job descriptions or skill sets. The merger document will need to include a plan for staff, which means going through a staff adjustment discernment process.

The document might also include procedural steps, such as permission for trustees to hire a lawyer and a budget for this and other necessary expenditures.

A merger of two or more meetings probably won't be approved all at once. The meetings will have to find sense of the meeting multiple times, each time proceeding a step or two further. Friends might be able to approve only one or two paragraphs at a time or might need to return to the document every few months.

Be as honest as possible about what will change. It can be tempting to encourage Friends to move forward by saying that "not much will change." But the truth is, in merging meetings, a lot will change, possibly including things that Friends like very much just the way they are. If we set an expectation that things can stay much the same, and then they do not, Friends are likely to stop attending the new community and drift away.

Combining or Merging Meetings

Check for inconsistencies between theory and action. As the merger document is being assembled, check to see whether it actually seems to reflect the relationship that Friends have envisioned. If the original plan was for one meeting to come under the care of another, is that care relationship materializing? If the original plan was two meetings joining together as separate preparative meetings in a new monthly meeting, do the property and staff and budget decisions reflect an appropriate power relationship between the two groups? This is about making sure that the practical steps explained in the document reflect the spiritual discernment of the meetings.

Approve the merger. This final approval of the merger document will probably come in the context of a combined business meeting, although it can be done separately. If the merging meetings make the final approval together, it's important that there are no surprise changes in the document at the final gathering. Friends should not be presented with anything they have not already had the opportunity to express concerns and ask questions about.

Square away the legal matters and move into the new facility. This single step can represent an enormous amount of time, energy, and possibly money. It's the execution of the merger document that the meeting approved. The Friends who are responsible for this execution will almost certainly run into snags. Buildings will need extra repairs. A new document of incorporation will spend weeks sitting on a state bureaucrat's desk. We can only expect the unexpected and try to maintain sufficient financial and spiritual reserves to deal with each problem as it comes. Friends will be more patient if they receive regular progress reports and the steps are transparent and easily understood. It will also help if the communities continue relationship-building work by worshiping together (or visiting each other's meetings for worship) and by holding joint social and service events.

Celebrate with worship and something festive. Eventually, the day will come when the merger is complete. Friends can celebrate this event with a special meeting for worship, inviting the neighborhood and Friends from the regional or yearly meeting to join the group. After worship, consider some additional way of celebrating the day—games, music, food, a nature walk, or whatever feels like an authentic celebration to your new community.

For the first few years, be careful about committee representation. If the newly combined meeting has also combined all or part of its committee structure, it will help to pay attention to representation on these committees for a little while. If, for example, two meetings have merged into a single meeting (rather than one meeting coming under the care of the other), committees with significant influence should have 50/50 representation from the two groups—even if one group was originally smaller than the other. This will help ensure that no one feels one group is being overshadowed by the other. After about five years, we can hope that everyone will feel entirely part of the new meeting, and no one will be concerned about representation dynamics of the old groups anymore.

A crucial piece of merging meetings is sacrificing our existing power dynamics. A merger is such a significant change that no existing formal or informal power structure is likely to survive it without some disruption. For those who have power in the meetings (because they hold particular committee positions, or because their grandfather donated the building, or because they understand the system better than anyone else, or because Friends know them well and tend to defer to their judgment) will need to release that power because it will not exist in the same form in the newly merged meeting. The transition becomes a learning experience about faith and mutual trust, in which we will find new ways of working and living together. The new ways may even be better than what we had before, but they will be less familiar and probably less comfortable, at least at first. Each open conversation and step toward building relationships will help us move through this transition.

Restructuring the Local Meeting

GENERALLY SPEAKING, A LOCAL meeting will consider restructuring when committee and staff adjustments are not enough. If the meeting's active membership has declined swiftly or significantly, or if the financial situation has become extremely precarious, the local meeting might no longer be structured appropriately as a monthly meeting.

Most local faith communities that are "monthly meetings" are called that because they gather for business once a month. A monthly meeting also holds membership, has a legal status as a distinct entity, conducts marriages and memorial meetings, maintains financial investments (even they're small, like a bank account), and owns or rents property. Some monthly meetings also employ staff.

If meeting for worship is still strong, or if the meeting has strong community or neighborhood ministries, then the meeting might not be ready be laid down, even if it can't manage the essential functions of a monthly meeting. In these cases, the meeting might consider restructuring. It could become an executive meeting, a preparative meeting, a worship group, and/or a house church.

These four models do not have uniform definitions throughout the Religious Society of Friends. Some yearly meetings have some of these types of meetings but not others. Some yearly meetings give conflicting definitions of the terms or have other types of designations. In this book, though, I'm going to give each of the terms a distinct definition and speak as though it is universally accepted. I do this simply to make the potential models easy to understand. In the end, what we call each model matters very little.

An *executive meeting* has the same legal and Quaker status as a monthly meeting, but it meets for business "as necessary" rather than monthly—usually, less often than monthly. Holding fewer meetings for business does take some pressure off Friends, allowing for more spiritual energy to go toward other purposes, but it doesn't solve big problems unless the meeting also simplifies in other ways, such as by focusing on one ministry and letting others go, or by hiring staff, or by selling the meetinghouse.

A *preparative meeting* is under the care of a monthly meeting and joins that meeting for business meetings. It may not have its own clerk, and if it does, the clerk role is simpler. A preparative meeting might not have a complete committee structure, but Friends in the preparative meeting may serve in roles of the monthly meeting's committee structure. It does not own property and usually is not a legal entity and does not hold funds. It may have a budget, but the income and expenditures of the preparative meeting ultimately flow through the bank accounts of the monthly meeting.

When a meeting becomes a preparative meeting, it has much less work to do. It can simplify its committee structure, it is not responsible for maintaining its property, and it does not need anyone to track its investments.

But a preparative meeting also loses some autonomy. Discernment becomes the responsibility of the monthly meeting, which certainly includes the Friends in the preparative meeting but also includes a number of other Friends. Because the preparative meeting is not entirely responsible for its assets, it also does not make independent decisions about the use of those assets.

In making the transition to a preparative meeting, Friends also must find a monthly meeting that is able to take it under its care. This may be difficult, especially if the preparative meeting wants to continue worshiping in its current building and if that property requires considerable attention.

A *worship group* is also under the care of a monthly meeting, but worship groups have much simpler structure than preparative meetings do. Worship groups gather only for worship and social time. This is a useful model for a local meeting that still has deep worship but is no longer able to conduct other types of meeting affairs.

Like a preparative meeting, a worship group is under the care of a monthly meeting. Worship groups do not hold separate membership, do not have clerks or committee structures, do not own property, are not legal entities, and do not hold funds. When a meeting transitions to being a worship group, all members transfer their membership to the monthly meeting. From a legal point of view, the worship group is not a separate entity at all from the monthly meeting, but it is distinct in practice because Friends continue to worship separately. Most commonly, Friends would form a worship group (rather than simply merging with the larger monthly meeting) either because the two groups have different worship styles or because it would be geographically difficult to come together for worship every week. Though it would be theoretically possible for a meeting to become a worship group and continue worshiping in its previous building (transferring the deed to the monthly meeting), it is more common for a worship group to gather in a rented or free public space or in a home.

A *house church* can be a preparative meeting or a worship group or even a monthly meeting, but it gathers in a private home—either the same one every time or different homes in rotation. A house church doesn't own property, and its need for funding is generally low. House churches tend to build powerful community among their members. However, they are limited in size by definition (according to how many Friends can fit in the home or yard), and they can feel intimidating to newcomers.

How does a local meeting find the right fit when restructuring? It's possible that Friends will feel an immediate resonance with one of the above models, but if the way forward isn't clear, there are some specific steps that help.

Start with what is working well in the meeting. If worship is strong but community ministries are not, it makes sense to preserve the worship. If many neighborhood organizations are using the building, the meeting will need to find a way to keep that going—either by maintaining the building or by turning it over to someone who can. If much of the meeting's community life connects to singing, it may be important to worship in a place with a piano. And so forth.

Identify where the meeting is struggling. In what way is the structure no longer supporting the community? Is there a budget shortfall? Does the building consume too many resources? Are there too many committee positions and not enough Friends to fill them? Are Friends in the meeting aging and needing much more pastoral care than they used to?

It might be useful to create a statement to help frame the meeting's discernment. "We need a structure for our meeting that will preserve _____ and _____, because those are things about our meeting that are working well and feel Spirit-led. But we also need a structure that will solve _____ and _____, because those problems are too much for us to deal with under our current structure."

Be aware of all the options. A meeting that is restructuring is likely to reference many sections of this book. Restructuring will almost always involve multiple changes—not just a shift from a monthly meeting to a preparative meeting, but also changing the committee structure and making staff transitions. Or not just a shift from a monthly meeting to a worship group, but also selling the property. Friends are searching for the combination of institutional adaptations that will allow the meeting to thrive—preserving what God is still calling the meeting to do while eliminating structural problems or reducing them to a manageable size.

Use open discussions and threshing sessions. A concept such as restructuring is too complicated to work through only in business meetings. Open discussions (in which Friends can ask questions and suggest alternatives) and threshing sessions (in which Friends listen to one another deeply in the context of open worship, without the intention of making a decision) are useful tools in developing and working through possibilities.

It's important to include distant members of the meeting and others who may feel attached to it even though they are not regularly present for worship. These Friends should receive notification as early as possible about the restructuring discernment process, and they should be given a pathway by which they can participate in that discernment process, even if it's not possible for them to be present for all gatherings. Otherwise, such Friends are likely to hear about big changes in the meeting at the last minute, which will cause hurt feelings at least and, possibly, serious conflict and disruption in the transition process.

Friends in the regional and yearly meeting will also need to know about the discernment process. Sometimes, they will be helpful, providing practical or spiritual resources to the local meeting. Other times, they will simply need early warning about a possible transition in order to feel prepared for it. This step is extremely important if a meeting is considering becoming a preparative meeting or worship group under the care of another meeting. In those cases, not only will the other meeting need the opportunity to participate in the discernment process (and undertake one of its own), but the action might require regional or yearly meeting approval.

Define the procedural steps and find sense of the meeting. A local meeting that is significantly restructuring might find it useful to establish a "restructuring document." This is not a legal contract but an internal document designed as a written record of what is proposed and what is approved. The document might include the new status of the meeting, definition of the care relationship (if one exists), and a plan for property transitions, staff transitions, and legal transitions.

If the local meeting is becoming a preparative meeting or worship group and will be under the care of another meeting (usually a meeting with monthly meeting status), the document should define that care relationship. What is required on the part of each group? What is thought to be desirable but is not strictly required? Where will membership be held? Who will be responsible for conducting marriages and memorial meetings? Who will own the property, and who will make decisions about it? Who will own the financial assets, and who will make decisions about them? Where and how often will business meetings be held? Who can serve each group in what sorts of roles—for example, could someone from the preparative meeting serve as clerk of the monthly meeting? Will the groups hold joint social events? Who has direct care of which neighborhood ministries?

Part of the reason for developing a restructuring document is to avoid the need to approve every detail simultaneously. It may be easier to find sense of the meeting about a few paragraphs at a time. When there are sections that Friends are not ready to approve, we can make notes about the outstanding questions and work further on them before the next business meeting.

Throughout the restructuring process, it will be important to make space for grief. The meeting is not dying, but it is aging, and it is not capable of doing everything it used to do. It's normal for Friends to experience feelings of frustration and nostalgia, possibly even anger. In addition to making explicit space for naming these feelings, it can help to name some of the gifts of the meeting's new phase of life: an ability to focus more on worship, simplicity, wisdom, and deep love between members of the community.

When the transition is finally complete, Friends may enjoy inviting others for a celebration of the meeting's first post-restructuring meeting for worship. Friends from the regional meeting or yearly meeting can contribute to a sense of gratitude and recognition.

Taking a Meeting "Under Our Care"

Friends often use the phrase "under the care of." Marriages are under the care of a monthly meeting. Missions are under the care of an organization. Schools or universities are sometimes under the care of a regional or yearly meeting. We don't always define this phrase very carefully, but it marks a spiritual relationship with practical implications.

In some ways, we can use a parent-child analogy to understand what it means to have something "under our care." We are responsible for making sure that anything under our care is nurtured, supported, held accountable, and able to thrive. We provide practical help, prayer, and ongoing loving relationship. But unlike the relationship between most parents and children, we do not assume that what is under our care is fundamentally less capable than we are, even in the beginning. Having something "under our care" does not imply a power imbalance. It only implies a particular sort of spiritual relationship.

In many parts of the world, Friends have enormous numbers of meetings that are nearing the end of their life cycles. Many of these meetings may eventually look for another group to take them "under their care." They will do this because they are no longer able to take on tasks like management of property, looking after financial assets, processing membership applications, and conducting monthly business. None of this is an indication that the individual Friends involved are lacking or inferior in some way. However, just as is true of individuals who age, meetings that age eventually become unable to do everything they used to do.

Historically, care relationships between meetings have usually been established in the first half of a meeting's life cycle, much like young parents having a child. A meeting in the maturity or stability phase would plant a worship group, and the worship group eventually became a preparative meeting, then a monthly meeting. In this scenario, the monthly meeting had the smaller meeting under its care temporarily. It nurtured the smaller meeting as it grew and then, eventually, recognized that the smaller meeting had become its own entity.

I believe we need to recognize that many meetings also need extra care and support at the end of their lives. A meeting that restructures itself into a worship group is probably nearing a time when it will be laid down. But that time is not yet, and the meeting still has holy work to do. It's vital in such a circumstance not to treat the relationship as if it is one between a parent and a child. The aging meeting has fully developed gifts, a rich history, and much wisdom to contribute, and these dynamics must be honored.

If planting new meetings is a bit like parenting, then a meeting finding help at the end of its life cycle is a bit like an elderly person needing assistance. In many cases, an aging individual will receive needed help from his or her own child, who is by that time an independent adult. Although not every family situation unfolds this way, the existing parent-child relationship and history makes a person's own offspring an obvious source of assistance in old age. We do not have a parallel dynamic for meetings. Many Quaker meetings have never had direct worship group "offspring." Even if they have, there's no guarantee that those "offspring" meetings will be in a position to take the aging meeting under their care. Therefore, many aging meetings will be searching for a group to take them under their care—and there will not be a self-evident place to start.

If we follow historical models, monthly meetings are the groups that must take preparative meetings or worship groups under their care. But in many places, there aren't many strong monthly meetings that are in a position to take another group under their care, which makes me wonder if we need to consider a new model. Could a regional meeting or a yearly meeting take a worship group directly under its care? We'd need to think carefully about how membership and pastoral care would work under those circumstances, but I don't see any reason we shouldn't experiment with this. In fact, I suspect we may have to.

What do we do if *we* are the meeting that is asked to take another meeting under our care? What are the implications for us? It might not be obvious what the other meeting is really asking for. In fact, the other meeting might not be sure what it's asking for. We have very few models for this type of transition—a meeting restructuring into a preparative meeting or worship group and coming under the care of another meeting—because it hasn't usually been done. Historically, most meetings have continued as monthly meetings until they lay themselves down. When that happens, the meeting often spends its last years barely managing, or not managing, to meet its basic obligations. What I'm proposing here is a new model, and it would take some trial and error to find the best ways forward.

If we take another meeting under our meeting's care, the first commitment is to *relationship*. We're agreeing to love the Friends in the other meeting. It's the type of love we have for near-neighbors or extended family, which does not necessarily require liking each other but definitely requires commitment and compromise. To love the other meeting, we must know the other meeting, which means visitation. We'll also commit to sharing our corporate discernment with the extended group. Worship groups and preparative meetings participate in monthly meeting for business with the monthly meeting under whose care they are, which means we are both expanding our agenda (to include matters related to both groups) and expanding our attendance list (which sometimes has the effect of making discernment longer. . .though also richer). If we take a meeting under our care, we are accepting its members as our members, and each of its new members will have a clearness committee that includes someone from our meeting. We're also entering a mutual service relationship, in which some committees will be populated by a combination of Friends from our meeting and the new meeting, and in which less formal service (such as work days or neighborhood ministries) will often become a combined effort.

Our second commitment is to *nurture*. We will worship with Friends from the new meeting as part of ongoing occasional visitation. We will pray for them. Although Friends from the worship group or preparative meeting will most often provide pastoral care for one another, we will step in if needed—for example, if several members of the worship group experience simultaneous health crises. If Friends from the worship group or preparative meeting are led to marry, those marriages will be under our care. We will also have care of the Friends' memorial meetings. It's not that Friends from the new meeting won't work on their own marriages and memorial meetings—of course they will—but if that meeting is under our care, we are all part of the same whole, so we will be responsible for these events, too.

Our third commitment is to *support*. If the new meeting is becoming a worship group, it will turn over its financial assets and property to us, and it will dissolve its legal identity as a separate entity. (If it is becoming a preparative meeting, it will probably take these same steps, though not for certain.) Our finance committee is now managing new funds and approving an additional budget—and probably has members from the worship group. Our buildings and grounds committee is now managing an additional property, possibly miles away from our own—and probably has members from the worship group. And our legal umbrella is expanding to include the new meeting, which means we may need to reconsider questions related to insurance and trustees. If the new meeting has a financial shortfall, it is our financial shortfall. If the new meeting has a legal problem, it is our legal problem.

The fourth commitment we make is *accountability*. If we agree to take a meeting under our care, we must define the relationship very carefully, and we must expect to hold the new meeting accountable to what has been agreed—and expect to be held accountable, ourselves, to that same agreement. We will also find ourselves in the same mutual accountability relationship that we are in with other Friends in our meetings: a sacred responsibility to seek and name and nurture one another's spiritual gifts, and to tell each other the truth with love.

The final commitment we make is providing the new meeting with *space to thrive*. We provide relationship, nurture, support, and accountability, but we do not attempt to make the new meeting's decisions for it. Matters that affect only the worship group or the preparative meeting can be discerned by only the worship group or the preparative meeting. We are in a committed relationship, but we are not in charge of that committed relationship. God is, and as much as possible, we respect the smaller meeting's discernment about its own future.

In other words, taking a meeting under our care is not an insignificant commitment. But nor should we move forward or decline on the basis of a cost-benefit analysis. This is a matter for spiritual discernment.

Are we led to be in relationship with this meeting? In most cases, of course, we already are in some form of relationship with the other meeting. They might be part of our region or part of our yearly meeting. But what we're talking about now is more direct relationship. At this point in our discernment, it's not necessary to worry much about how things will work out, from a practical point of view, or exactly how we'll define the relationship. The question is simply whether we're led to be in any kind of relationship. Lloyd Lee Wilson once said that the first call to travel in ministry is the experience of love for a group of Friends not present. That might be a good indication in discerning this sort of relationship, as well. Does our meeting experience love for that group of Friends not present?

Is the proposed care relationship the right relationship? It is possible that we will be led to be in relationship with the other meeting but that we are not led to take it under our care. Perhaps we'll be led to spiritual accompaniment, in which we regularly pray for and visit the other meeting. Perhaps we'll be led to a gift of financial resources, especially if we ourselves have an excess. Or perhaps we'll be led to propose a merger of the two meetings, which may be quite different from a care relationship.

Can we find a collective sense of the meeting about how we will define the care relationship? This is the step that includes an enormous amount of work and probably quite a lot of time. Within our own meeting, and working together with the other meeting, we must settle any number of questions. As we're working on the answers, it might help to develop the relationship between our two meetings. We might hold occasional combined meetings for worship. We could have community work days or play days together. We may set up small study groups that include Friends from each meeting. We could pray for one another, as well.

Here are some of the questions that must be explored:

Who will visit whom, and how often, in order to maintain a strong relationship between the meetings? Will the visitation be formalized, or will Friends simply be encouraged to do it as led?

Are we able to commit to collective discernment as a single monthly meeting? Where will business meetings be held? Who will set the agenda, and how?

Will the memberships of Friends be transferred to the monthly meeting? Will this happen automatically, or will Friends have to request transfers of membership? What will happen if a new Friend requests membership in the worship group or preparative meeting?

Does either meeting have recorded ministers? If so, who will hold the recordings? What does that mean?

How will Friends participate in service to the meeting(s)? Which committees or volunteer roles will be combined, and which will be kept separate? How will Friends be chosen or volunteer for service?

Do either of the meetings employ staff? Will the scope of the staff member's job description change? Who is responsible for paying the staff? Who will supervise the staff?

Taking a Meeting "Under Our Care"

Is each group solely responsible for its own pastoral care, or is there a mutual relationship between the groups? How will one group ask for help from the other if help is needed?

Who will form clearness committees for marriages? Where will marriages be held? Under whose care will the marriages be, and what does that mean?

Who will be responsible for arranging memorial meetings and writing memorial minutes? Where will memorial meetings be held?

Who will make decisions about the management of funds? Is either meeting in debt? How will each group be supported financially? Are there restrictions on how the funds can be spent? Are these legal restrictions or restrictions that we ourselves have placed?

How will the property be managed? Will the meeting now have one building or two? What about burial grounds? If any property will be sold in the transition, who will be responsible for managing this? What will happen to any proceeds?

Does either meeting have ongoing neighborhood or world ministries? Will anything about the management of these change?

Who is responsible for making sure that the necessary legal steps are taken? Will we hire a lawyer to help us? Who will pay for this? Will everyone be appropriately insured under our current policies? If not, what changes need to be made?

What will happen in the future if some part of this care relationship isn't working well? If we're experiencing problems in our relationship, how will we handle them? Will we check in regularly to see how everyone is feeling about the situation? Will difficulties be discussed in business meetings or in some other setting?

When all of these matters are settled, and if we still feel called to move forward, we can affirm the new relationship between the meetings in a combined meeting for business.

It's tempting, again, to look at the new relationship through the lens of a cost-benefit analysis. What will we gain in exchange for taking this meeting under our care? While I don't think that's the most helpful way of phrasing the question, I do believe there are potential blessings. The newly configured meeting will cover a wider geographic area. It will have greater diversity of gifts and experiences and a larger group with whom to celebrate joys and to whom we can turn when someone needs help. Moreover, if it is rightly led, it may grow into something we never expected that has always been part of God's plan.

Property

FRIENDS KNOW THAT GOD can be anywhere. All places are holy. There is nothing inherently sacred about our worship spaces—no consecration ceremony, no blessed objects dedicated to God. But despite this, we often feel a deep connection to the presence of God in some particular place.

When we have had spiritually transformative experiences in a given place, we almost always become attached to that place. Perhaps we grieved the loss of a close friend in the meetinghouse. Perhaps we experienced healing or convincement. Perhaps we were married in this building, or our child was, or we remember our grandchildren running up and down the aisles. All of these are powerful memories, and when these experiences become part of our spiritual rootedness, so does the building in which they occurred.

Nevertheless, what matters most is not the building. What matters most is our continued ability to connect with God, and if we leave the building, our memories of prior connections can come with us. It's possible for our love of a building (or outdoor space, or bench, or window) to become so intwined with our relationship with God that the love becomes idolatrous. If losing the physical space feels like losing God, idolatry may be an apt description.

Like all other parts of our institutional structure, the physical space in which we worship should be supporting our community's ability to be faithful. If, instead, our community has become dedicated to supporting the physical space, we have gotten things backwards. It's time to reassess our relationship with our property.

There are a number of signs that it's time for such a reassessment. Do we have a growing inability to keep up with the care and maintenance of the property? Are we focusing less on ministry and mutual care because our property requires so much of our attention and money? Is the building used much less than it used to be?

There are less obvious signs, too, that it may be time to consider making a change. We might be experiencing a general sense of pessimism that clouds our decision-making, or there may be growing anxiety or fatalism about the future of our meeting. These are symptoms of a spiritual condition that is stuck, without much hope of moving forward, and it's often because so much of time, energy, and money is pouring into our building, but we aren't ready or able to make a change.

Another sign is a growing disconnect between the Friends in the meeting and the neighborhood community. Do we know the people in the neighborhood? Are we in relationship with them? If not, why is our meeting still physically located here?

Reassessing our relationship with our building does not necessarily mean selling, though it might. It will probably help not to pose the initial question as "should we sell our property?" but as "what relationship does God call us, now, to have with this property?"

The first phase of property-related discernment will probably be information-gathering. There are three parts to this exploration: the meeting community, the meetinghouse, and the meeting neighborhood.

The meeting community. To what ministries are we primarily led as a meeting? What are the most important concerns that God has given us to carry together—not as individual Friends, but as a group? How much energy do we have? How much time and money do we have? What is important to each of us about our meeting community? How do we feel about the state of our meeting community right now?

The meetinghouse. What are the characteristics of this property? What are the best things about it? What are the worst things about it? Does it need significant repairs? Are there legal restrictions on how it can be changed or used? For what purposes does it lend itself? What is its approximate monetary value? Are there any funds that are legally dedicated to its upkeep?

The meeting neighborhood. Do we know the people in our neighborhood? If we go for a walk in the neighborhood, what do we see? What is thriving in this neighborhood? What is needed in this neighborhood? What do our neighbors wish would be done with this building?

When we discern the next steps for our property, the likely way forward will be somewhere in the intersection between what is best for the meeting community, what is best for the meeting neighborhood, and how the property can best serve those purposes. The needs of the meeting neighborhood matter as much as the needs of the meeting community because the property *is where it is*. It will not move, even if the meeting community does, so good stewardship involves asking, "What is God's purpose for the property in this place?" regardless of whether the meeting community will stay here.

In discernment, we might be called to *stay, but share the building*. Offering rentals or free use of space is a wonderful way to build our relationships with our neighborhood community, although it's unlikely to increase our numbers at worship on Sunday—and entering into relationships with that unspoken desire may be disingenuous. Sharing the building with people in the neighborhood also makes it more likely that the building will be used for purposes relevant to the neighborhood. But sharing can require considerable investment up front (if serious repairs are needed) and may add to maintenance costs. Even if people using the building are paying rent, this strategy is unlikely to solve a serious financial shortfall.

We might be called to *stay in the building but also sell it*. If the meeting community has a strong relationship with the neighborhood and is led to continue that relationship (and thus stay in place), this is an option that can solve a financial shortfall. The meeting would need to find another organization—probably another faith community, but possibly a nonprofit—that would be interested in purchasing the building while still allowing the meeting to worship in it. The trickiest part about this arrangement is adapting to the meeting's new relationship with the property. The new owners might redecorate the space. They might want to worship in the main room on Sunday mornings, and the meeting might need to change its worship time or use a different room in the building. How will it feel to stay in the same property but have it change in ways we can't control?

Another option, which might not always be obvious, is to *stay and find a creative solution*. The meeting might be able to sell its development rights or air rights, explore ground leases, get a grant, or find financial incentives offered as part of historic landmarking. These are options that work well if the problem is just financial, but they require an investment of time and energy (and hiring experts), so they are probably not the best way forward for a meeting that does not have enough people to take on as much labor as the building requires.

Sometimes a meeting can *sell (or give away) the property but have a transition period*. There might be another faith community or a nonprofit organization that is interested in the property but is not in a hurry, in which case there can be a temporary building-sharing situation for a year or two before the transfer is finalized and the meeting community moves elsewhere. This might help in making sure that the neighborhood community's needs are met, since there's time to experiment with a new group in the building before the change becomes permanent, but it does require sufficient money to support the slow transition. Also, if the meeting is considering giving its building to another group rather than selling it, it's important to pay attention to whether the building will actually be a blessing. If it requires a large investment for major repairs, it might become a burden for a fledgling meeting or nonprofit. A slow transition can offer everyone an opportunity to make sure the match is right.

Finally, the meeting might *sell (or give away) the building and move immediately*. In this situation, the meeting's financial problems can be solved relatively quickly, but there won't be much opportunity to control what happens to the building. The question may be one of what is most important: is it all right for the building to be turned into a parking lot if, in exchange, the meeting receives a large payment that can be used to support its ministries?

For meetings that are selling property (or making other significant changes in property use), I strongly recommend the ecumenical book *Transitioning Older and Historic Sacred Places* by Rachel Hildebrant with Joshua Castaño. It contains excellent advice about assessing church property, hiring professionals, and many other practical considerations.

Friends are likely to love both their meeting communities and their meetinghouses, but we must remember that these are not the same. The building is meant to support our faithfulness; we are not meant to sacrifice in order to support the building. When it's time to move on, we can offer thanks for the building's presence in our lives and step forward to what is next in faithfulness.

Laying Down a Meeting

ALL MEETINGS, LIKE ALL people, will die. Local faith communities last about a hundred years, on average. An exceptionally long-lasting Quaker meeting might go on for several hundred years. But eventually, all meetings will go through the stages of the life cycle in a more or less sequential fashion and will reach a stage that we can call death. In that stage, the meeting might still gather for worship, but it's not able to do anything else, nor does it have sufficient energy to revive itself.

Meetings are not automatically laid down when they reach this final stage. They can exist in a legal form for many years, even if all of the meeting's Friends die or stop attending. At this point, the meeting has become a ghost meeting, with legal complications (and possibly assets) for someone else to deal with because the meeting can no longer do this for itself.

Just as many humans tend to avoid talking about or preparing for death, meetings tend to say, "We're not finished. We're still here. Maybe God will even help us grow again." I believe that God can and does perform miracles, but the miracles we receive are not always the ones we hoped for. At the end of a meeting's life cycle, the miracle might be the Friends who gather around to show their love for the meeting, or the deeply gathered worship we encounter in discerning our ending, or the new church we're able to bless with our property. It might be learning stories about the history of our meeting that we never knew before, as we sort through the archives. It might be something we never see, some new thing that is born twenty years later because we released the necessary spiritual or financial energy to nurture it.

As people can, a meeting can plan for its end before it has actually reached it. It might talk about its eventual end, plan for how the institutional change will happen, and then not need to act on the plan for another six years. When the time comes, it might sell its property (as previously discerned), move to a rental space, and continue for another five years, then transition to a worship group, come under the care of another meeting, and continue for eight years more before laying itself down. Those final nineteen years are not prolonging the end; they are evidence of the meeting faithfully responding to changing conditions and preparing for a time when it will be laid down. They will probably be nineteen truly precious, life-changing years.

How do we know when a meeting is nearing its end? It's very likely we'll know on a spiritual level. We'll sense something old and tired in the spirit of the meeting. We'll look around us and see that the Friends in our community, however much they love each other and the meeting, cannot keep it going. But if specific, practical signs are helpful in assessing, here are some to watch for:

The meeting is no longer capable of taking on its *essential functions*, such as weekly worship, meetings for business, relationships with the regional or yearly meetings, and arranging memorials or marriages.

Friends focus on *survival, not ministry,* when they discuss the meeting's future.

The *average attendance at worship is shrinking.*

All, or nearly all, Friends are *past retirement age,* possibly even in their late seventies and above.

Friends struggle to provide *mutual care* because so many Friends need help and so few have the resources or ability to provide it.

The meeting's focus is primarily internal, and it's difficult or impossible to take on *ministry outside the walls* of the meetinghouse, such as neighborhood or world ministries.

The meeting is not *vital*—does not experience the presence of God in worship—or is not *viable*—does not have the financial or human resources to keep itself going.

When a meeting lays itself down, it has the opportunity to consider its legacy. What will happen to the meeting's assets? What will happen to the meeting's story, and how will it be shared? Friends are a resurrection people, but resurrection is not the same as resuscitation. How might your meeting have new or continued life after its death? What might God do that can't be done here?

Laying down a meeting is almost never a failure. Usually, a meeting reaches the end of its life cycle as part of the natural course of things, and there's nothing anyone could have done to change it. In these cases, laying down the meeting is the most faithful response available to the meeting's condition. It doesn't belittle anything that came before. It is simply what happens next in the story.

Sometimes, a meeting reaches the end of its life cycle because of a significant external disruption or internal conflict. This can be especially heart-breaking. Friends find themselves thinking, "If we could have done things differently. . ." And that may be true. But even if so, we can't go back in time and change things. If laying down the meeting is the most faithful available response to conditions now, then laying down the meeting is not a failure. We might regard what came before as a failure, and if that's the case, we can only strive for forgiveness of ourselves and others. This reminds me of my favorite definition of that word: "Forgiveness is giving up all hope of a better past."

What are the steps to laying down a meeting?

Say it out loud. Someone has to speak the words: "We might be called to lay down the meeting." This can be a hard thing to say. Friends who find the idea alarming may react in anger or behave dismissively. But it's also possible that Friends will be relieved, especially if they've been hoping someone else would say it first.

Commit to Spirit-led discernment. We should neither lay down the meeting nor keep it going just because we think it's the right idea. Friends believe that we can always receive guidance from God, and that does not change because our meeting is nearing the end of its life cycle. If we commit to deep listening and corporate discernment, which means trusting each other, we can find way forward.

Worship. The question of whether to lay down a meeting is an especially good one to hold in worship, and not only in the context of business meetings. It can also be held in prayer during normal meetings for worship. If a query or quotation would be helpful as a starting place, and if one cannot be found about the laying down of a meeting, consider using queries or quotes about end-of-life concerns for people. This metaphorical framework can be very useful.

Talk about it. In facilitated conversations and in open conversations, talk about the possibility of laying down the meeting. How does it feel? How will Friends know when it's time? Simple, back-and-forth conversation helps us work through things in a manner that is different from formal business meetings, although both are important.

Let distant and less-active community members know what's being considered. More Friends care about a meeting than are immediately obvious. Some Friends may have moved away; others may have stopped attending but appreciate knowing the meeting is available. If such Friends don't know that the meeting is considering laying itself down, or if no meaningful pathway is available for them to be involved in the discernment process, they might appear at the last minute wanting to "save" the meeting, which can be painful for everyone.

Talk with the regional or yearly meeting. Friends in the regional or yearly meeting may have experience with laying down meetings. They might be able to help. Even if no one can provide direct assistance, we know that no Quaker meeting functions as an island. We are part of a broader covenant community, and part of being in relationship is sharing honestly about our condition. There may also be times when, if Friends in the regional or yearly meeting aren't involved in or aware of the discernment process, they may push against the meeting laying itself down, perhaps believing that this is helpful or inspiring when, actually, they are simply reacting to the societal concepts of "more is better" and "endings are failures," neither of which is fundamentally true.

Hold threshing sessions for concerns, grief, and joys. A threshing session is a period of open worship in which Friends are invited to express their feelings, their thoughts, and their leadings regarding a potential change. Threshing sessions are different from business meetings because no decision is anticipated. They are purely for the purpose of listening and being listened to. Beginning a threshing session with queries can help guide Friends' speaking. These can be simple, even something like, "Are we called to lay down the meeting? How does the possibility feel to you? Are there specific things you're concerned about as we discern our next steps? Does anything feel hopeful about the possibility of laying down the meeting?"

Find sense of the meeting. Eventually, it will be time to find sense of the meeting. Sometimes Friends will first approve laying down the meeting, then work through the logistics of how to do it. Other times, Friends will need to approve the logistics and steps, then will be able to approve laying down the meeting. Neither way is wrong, and whichever order seems to work better for the group is probably the order in which to go.

Before the Resurrection

Consider the meeting's legacy. What has the meeting already left behind for future generations? What more might the meeting feel called to leave behind, and how? This stage is both a reflection on the meeting's history and a chance to figure out how the meeting will live on after its ending. Nearly all meetings will have some assets when they reach the end of their life cycles. Some will have significant financial or real estate assets. Grounded, Spirit-led corporate discernment can be especially difficult when we're talking about wealth. Suddenly, a lot of human nature enters the conversation, including diverse attitudes about money and differing priorities and leadings among Friends. A helpful question might be, "What has always been important to this meeting, throughout our history?" That framing can encourage Friends to consider the meeting's legacy as a continuation of its existing story rather than an entirely new piece of discernment.

Care for one another during the transition. Friends will need time to feel and express grief. Any loss of the familiar incites grief, and loss of the beloved especially so. Grief includes sadness, anger, denial, fear, and more, and not all Friends will experience the same emotions at the same time, nor to the same degree. Spending time together and working together as a community will require patience.

Each Friend in the community will also need a new worship home. There are many possibilities for this. Some Friends may be moving. Others may join another meeting, either in person or online. Other Friends might decide to worship with a different faith community. Some groups may continue to worship together informally even though the meeting itself has been laid down. What matters most is not checking logistical boxes but making sure that no one feels cast adrift.

Meeting communities are composed of Friends with interpersonal relationships, and though these relationships are supported by meeting activities, they don't have to end when the meeting ends. Do Friends want to stay in touch? How will Friends do this? There might be a monthly dinner or prayer partners or one Friend who agrees to send out an occasional group email. Having some plan for ongoing contact is important, even if the plan changes over time, because it's all too easy to agree "we'll stay in touch" and then, if no one takes initiative, for each Friend to doubt whether others really wanted that connection.

Documenting Friends' memories is another form of caring for one another. This can happen in whatever form is easiest: collecting photos, writing stories, recording video or audio, and so forth. The archive itself may be useful for future generations, but the very act of making the archive and telling the stories also provides time for reflection and gratitude.

Take on the practical and legal tasks. An early step is to check the yearly meeting's book of discipline. There may be a specific process for laying down a meeting, and if so, this should be followed as closely as possible so as not to surprise or confuse anyone.

Separate from the Quaker process is the legal process required by a meeting's nation, state, or town. If the meeting is incorporated as a nonprofit or charity, there may be legal requirements for the dispensation of assets already included in the establishing documents. Even smaller items, like hymnals or furniture, can't be given directly to Friends from the meeting if they legally belong to the meeting itself—but it is possible to hold a sale open to the public in which Friends can purchase such things for a reasonable price. Otherwise, check with a lawyer. It's likely that everything that belongs to the meeting must be donated or sold in accordance with local law and the meeting's establishing documents.

Minutes and membership records should be archived for future historical research. Many yearly meetings, though not all, have a specific process in place for archival materials. The archive (and there are different archives that focus on different Quaker groups) will have specific policies about what's wanted and in what format, so it may take some time and some conversations to learn what should be sent, how, and to where.

If the meeting has physical property, it will need to discern what should happen to that property. When possible, the discernment process can include non-Friends who live or work in the neighborhood. What do they believe the neighborhood most needs in the building or on the land? Because the property itself will not move or disappear, the preferences of people in the local area are directly relevant to the property's future.

Mark the meeting's end with a memorial. Just as we honor human life with memorial practices, we can honor a meeting's life as it reaches its ending. Friends might gather for a memorial meeting for worship for the meeting itself, using open worship to speak about how God's presence has been felt in the meeting. In some cases, Friends might write a memorial minute, documenting the historical activities of the meeting and sharing this with other Friends and possibly the neighborhood community.

If the meeting's assets or property have been transferred to a new faith community, nonprofit organization, or other group, the memorial can also celebrate this. The receiving community might want a formal opportunity

Before the Resurrection

to express gratitude or to tell the story of what they anticipate will be done with the assets. In this way, Friends can remember that the impact of the meeting will live on, even though the institution itself is ending.

On Archives

THE WRITTEN NARRATIVE OF a meeting—its minutes, its founding documents, its membership records, and so forth—is the story of how God's presence has been felt. For this reason, the process of archiving the records is a spiritual practice. It's akin to the customs of Old Testament patriarchs, who often built stone altars to mark places where God had done some particular thing. By constructing a marker and naming it after God's actions, they ensured that everyone who passed would remember God's power.

Especially in times of institutional transition, archiving the meeting's story can address spiritual needs in addition to practical ones. Friends who record their memories have a built-in opportunity to reflect, to express gratitude, and to grieve. It is a way of honoring the past of the meeting as well as a path for transmitting knowledge to the future.

Most, but not all, yearly meetings have a procedure in place for archiving historical materials. If your yearly meeting cannot provide guidance, Swarthmore College in Pennsylvania is an excellent source for information about best archival practices, including what to keep, where it might be sent, and in what format it should best be stored.

Pastoral Care in Transitions and Endings

NEARLY ALL INSTITUTIONAL ADAPTATIONS will provoke feelings of grief. This might seem counterintuitive, especially because the meeting's new structure is theoretically better than the old one and will lighten Friends' workload and make space for meaningful ministries. But all change implies loss as we move away from the familiar. Even Abraham, when God promised to lead him to the promised land, first had to leave his father's house behind.

Nearly all of us are familiar with Elisabeth Kubler-Ross's stages of grief: denial, anger, bargaining, despair, and acceptance. And nearly all of us know that actual grief does not proceed in an orderly or predictable fashion. The five stages may all be present as a meeting transitions, but Friends will not all experience the stages at the same time or to the same degree.

I've spoken a lot, in earlier parts of this book, about the various ways Friends express denial. "The meeting will grow if we just try harder to be welcoming. . .we've always had trouble finding members for the property committee, this is no different. . .three new families could show up next week. . .if we just get through this period of inflation, our budget will balance again." Denial is a powerful force, and Friends experiencing denial may undermine corporate discernment by refusing to acknowledge the existence of a problem.

Anger also appears in a variety of ways. "The trustees should have warned us about this. . .why am I the only one who's been talking about a budget shortfall for the last six years?. . .I'm just trying to keep the ministry and counsel committee going, and you're undermining my work by talking about transitions. . .if we'd sold the building when I said we needed to, we wouldn't be talking about closing now. . .I will hate myself if my generation is the one that fails our community. . .we'll become a worship group over my dead body." Many people experience anger as a reaction to injustice or loss of control, which makes it a very natural emotion during institutional adaptations. Often, even when we've agreed to them, changes feel random or undeserved. Unjust.

Friends often engage in bargaining as part of the corporate discernment process. This is what we're doing when we form working groups to study the problem but then don't accept their recommendations. We think perhaps we've done enough by forming the working group in the first place. Or maybe, when only two Friends can be found to serve on the budget committee, we go to the budget committee's handbook page and reduce the desired number of committee members from eight to five. This kind of institutional adaptation does nothing, but if we're trapped in a bargaining phase, we might hope it can be enough.

Friends will often express despair by acting as if the situation is hopeless. "There's no point making changes, nothing will make the meeting function. . .we can't possibly agree on what to do. . .Quakerism is dying. . .all social organizations are falling apart." As peculiar as it sounds, there's something comforting about hopelessness. It lets us off the hook. If we have no hope, there's no reason to try. We can comfortably run out the clock, telling ourselves, "We can't do anything about it anyway."

When Friends express acceptance, they are ready to make institutional changes, but they still must discern which changes are appropriate. This can't be done without space to grieve. Someone must create opportunities for one-on-one conversations, small group worship sharing, and threshing sessions, all of which give time for Friends to express and work through their emotions. These kinds of opportunities can happen formally or informally, scheduled or unscheduled, depending on what works best for the meeting community.

Good queries can support a grieving process, and worship sharing or threshing sessions ensure that Friends' responses to queries are listened to. At various times in an adaptation discernment process, Friends might ask each other questions such as the following:

Why did you first become part of this meeting?

What is one of your favorite memories of being in this building?

When we talk about change, what frightens you or makes you feel anxious?

Before the Resurrection

What is special about this meeting that shouldn't be lost?

I find it helpful, when I'm specifically trying to support grief conversations, to remind Friends to express their own emotions and not someone else's. A statement like, "Other people are scared of selling the building, but I'm not" is actually very unhelpful. Friends who fall into the category of "other people" may resent being labeled as 'scared' when they don't feel that way or haven't said so for themselves.

Friends who slip into this mode—talking about others' feelings or actions rather than their own—are often resisting vulnerability. Other times, they're trying to use their turn to speak to start an argument or express disapproval of what others have said. There are times when it's appropriate to work through conflict in a back-and-forth manner, but structured worship sharing and threshing sessions are not that time.

Occasionally, a Friend will need one-on-one pastoral care during a transition process, especially if that Friend is in a very different place emotionally or spiritually from the rest of the group. A personal visit from a pastor or a Friend on the ministry and counsel committee can provide a chance for the Friend to be heard without creating an unreasonable disruption in a group setting. Usually, a one-on-one visit will help the situation, especially if the Friend visiting is experienced in offering pastoral care. But sometimes, a Friend is specifically seeking attention and will become more disruptive to the group process, rather than less so, over time. The group may need to affirm the fundamental difference with something like, "We hear how much you want the meeting to do X instead of Y, but that is not the sense of the meeting. We are sorry we can't do what you so badly want us to do, but as of now, we will no longer be discussing that option."

When the meeting transitions (monthly meeting to worship group, previous building to new worship space, two meetings to one merged meeting, meeting laying itself down), a ceremony or celebration of some kind can be a vital part of pastoral care for the community. The substance of the event is less important than the act of acknowledging a significant change. It can be as simple as a special meeting for worship, in which favorite songs are sung or someone tells stories from the history of the meeting. If possible, it's nice to invite distant Friends, Friends who grew up in the meeting, people from the neighborhood, and/or Friends from the regional or yearly meeting to join the event. Doing so creates a deeper sense of connection, as the change is significant to the wider community.

Transitions and Endings for Regional Meetings

For the purposes of this book, I'm defining a regional meeting as an association of local meetings that is smaller than a yearly meeting. Historically, these were called quarterly meetings because they met four times each year. Today, in various parts of the world, they are regional meetings, area meetings, half-yearly meetings, and so on.

Centuries ago, regional meetings were essential. An annual gathering (yearly meeting) wasn't enough to build community among Friends and discern the will of God for the Society beyond local meetings, but it wasn't feasible to gather yearly meetings more frequently because of the travel required by horseback or buggy. Thus, quarterly meetings—a group with which to gather every three months, small enough for a horse to cross in a day.

Very few Friends ride horses now. But because we tend to lean on tradition, making changes only when a change is obviously needed, most of us still have regional meetings. The structure of these varies wildly. Some hold memberships. Some employ staff. Some have witness committees or do missions fundraising. Some own property or have vast financial resources. Some are primarily discernment groups, seasoning minutes from monthly meetings before they're sent to yearly meeting. Some are functioning as social groups. Some aren't functioning at all.

I'm speaking from the grapevine, not a quantitative study, but it seems as though most regional meetings are struggling. Like many local meetings today, they have difficulty filling committee slots or finding clerks.

Attendance at regional gatherings is low. Many Friends aren't sure why the regional meeting exists.

An exception to this pattern is regional meetings that are geographically distant from the population center of their yearly meetings. In these cases, the region itself might be very strong while the connection to the yearly meeting feels weak.

Friends, I suspect, are looking for connection beyond their local meetings, but the double layer (regional and then yearly meetings) is more than we need. This isn't categorically true, but in many cases, Friends spend time with their local meetings and their yearly meeting, skipping the middle step entirely. As a natural consequence, yearly meetings begin to do more, often gathering more than annually and providing various types of service and support directly to local meetings.

So why do we still have regional meetings?

Just as I've said about local meetings, I don't advocate for any regional meeting laying itself down if it's not led to do so. The meeting discerns its own future. That's an essential Quaker principle. There are regional meetings that should not be laid down because they are serving essential functions. They are vital (experiencing the presence and movements of the Holy Spirit) and viable (having plenty of human and financial resources to keep going).

Other regional meetings, I suspect, continue not because they're serving essential functions but because they are *supposed to be* serving essential functions. The yearly meeting's book of discipline might say that regional meetings are responsible for the health of local meetings, or care of pastors, or support for ministries, or seasoning of new proposals for the yearly meeting. And because all of these are important functions, no one suggests laying down or changing the regional meeting.

There is something deeply silly, and frankly also unfaithful, about perpetuating a system that's no longer working because its theoretical purpose is so important. If the purpose is important, and if the current system isn't serving that purpose in any real way, then we need to find a new way to serve that purpose.

Like local meetings, regional meetings might consider a wide variety of institutional adaptations: changing the committee structure, making staff transitions, moving to hybrid or online status, merging with other regional meetings, restructuring entirely, reassessing their relationship with property and finances, and laying themselves down. I want to acknowledge at the outset that according to many yearly meeting books of discipline, regional meetings don't have the ability to change most of these things. Doing so in the technically correct sense would require discernment by the whole yearly meeting, followed by a change to the book of discipline, followed by all regional meetings (most likely) restructuring in precisely the same way. The process would take years and would result in a new system that we couldn't be sure would actually work.

I suggest a different approach. Let's experiment.

I'm not advocating for regional meetings going rogue, and I hope that any regional meeting making significant changes would keep Friends in the yearly meeting up to date. But our circumstances have shifted enormously since we first established regional meetings, first with the invention of the automobile, then with the coming of internet access and email, and finally with the widespread use of videoconferencing technology. We have more than a century of adaptations to catch up on. We will have to try some things and find out what works.

Changing the committee structure. For some regional meetings, the primary problem is finding Friends to serve on committees. In this case, a good question might be, "Which of our committees are replicating work that is also being done in local meetings or by the yearly meeting?" We might discover that half the tasks in committees' job descriptions are duplications of work that is being done elsewhere. Perhaps a local meeting is already doing excellent adult religious education and is willing to invite Friends from elsewhere in the region to participate. Perhaps the yearly meeting is recognizing ministries. Perhaps an umbrella organization is supporting pastors. If the work is happening elsewhere, we don't need to replicate it—though we might need to serve as a communications channel so that local meetings can find the help they're looking for.

Once we know what functions are essential in the region, we can consider how best to fulfill these functions. Is a committee structure the best match? Or can we use working groups, task groups, or volunteer positions? Do we need to affirm a Friend's ministry? You can find much more detail about these options in an earlier section of this book, "Changing the Committee Structure."

Making staff transitions. A few regional meetings have extensive staff structures, and still more employ a staff member or two. But the majority have no staff at all.

After a regional meeting has checked for duplication of efforts and is clear what work needs to be done, it might discover there is still a shortage of Friends who are able to take on the work—either because there are not enough Friends available or because the available Friends don't have the right skill sets or spiritual gifts. In these cases, it might make sense to consider hiring a staff member.

When hiring staff for a regional meeting, Friends might consider whether support is most needed for the work of the region or for the work of the local meetings in the region. Should a staff position be designed to keep the regional meeting's institutional work going? Or should a staff position be designed to support the institutional work happening within each local meeting? The best approach will vary from region to region.

Either way, Friends must remember three basic principles: release of ministry, fair pay for fair effort, and appropriate support and accountability for staff.

Friends do not hire staff in a purely employer-employee relationship. We hope that our staff members are released ministers, meaning members of our community who feel called by God to take on the staff position and who are financially released so that they can focus on this work. In other words, we anticipate working alongside our staff and maintaining loving and equal interpersonal relationships with them.

Unfortunately, we sometimes associate ministry with sacrifice and expect released ministers to work very hard for comparatively little pay—and to be happy to do this. As a community, we are responsible for ensuring that our staff members are not expected to work more than the number of hours designated and that the financial compensation is fair. In new staff relationships, this might require tracking hours for the first few months and holding periodic check-in meetings to see whether the position is unfolding as intended.

Finally, if the staff member is a released minister, we are obliged to provide the sorts of support and accountability that are appropriate for ministry. This means that we allow the Friend in a staff position to fulfill the staff role as led, without micromanaging, and that we'll be receptive of the fruits of their ministry rather than critical by default. We will also provide a clear channel for spiritual and practical accountability, usually in the form of a small committee or line manager, and we will not attempt to establish additional accountability channels outside of what has been agreed.

Moving to hybrid or online status. In some regional meetings, the primary difficulty is attendance at meetings for business. This is especially likely to be a problem if most Friends in the region are elderly or have young children or if travel to regional meetings is long or difficult. Some regional meetings have addressed these problems with free childcare, carpooling, or social events before and after a business meeting, but we can also consider holding regional meetings as hybrid or online-only events.

Hybrid and online business meetings place additional burdens on the meeting's clerk and recording clerk. Maintaining a sense of spiritual groundedness and gathering a sense of the meeting can become difficult. Even practical matters are harder. Friends must focus on slowing down, taking turns, and ensuring that everyone can see and hear.

Successful hybrid and online gatherings will probably result in additional attendance, but the online elements also require more deliberate attention to building community. Friends will need to set aside small-group time for fellowship or worship sharing.

When groups gather online, a common side effect is a sense of distance from the geographic area. Friends who physically travel to regional gatherings will pass through cities or farms or small towns on the way. This will not happen for Friends who attend online, and we can lose an innate awareness of one another's life circumstances. If we do not visit one another's neighborhoods and meetinghouses, we may not understand one another's contexts. Neighborhood ministries might feel less relevant. Friends might join our regional gatherings from multiple time zones away.

We can respond to this natural distancing in a couple of ways. One is to reinforce our geographic connections by encouraging intervisitation, sharing photos, and practicing verbal and written storytelling about our neighborhoods and neighborhood ministries. The other is to embrace the nongeographic nature of the regional meeting, focusing primarily on the needs and the leadings of individual Friends or local meetings, possibly even accepting new local meetings into membership that are geographically far away.

Merging with other regional meetings. I know of several situations in which two or three regional meetings from the same yearly meeting are each struggling to manage their basic functions, generally because not enough Friends are available to take on positions of service. In situations where travel is not prohibitively long in the automobile age, such regions could simply merge. They might begin by worshiping and holding business together twice a year, perhaps spring and fall, while winter and summer gatherings continue to happen separately. Through experimentation, they might discover that certain committees or projects can merge. It might be possible to have just one clerk, or perhaps co-clerks, for the regions combined. In time, Friends might discover that it would be quite natural to merge into a single region, sharing resources and managing business together.

Moving forward incrementally, rather than merging all at once, would likely be easier for most regions, especially if the Friends don't know each other well or have some history of distrust. But in other cases, regions might be able to simply agree to combine, especially if neither region has complex property or financial situations. Merging eliminates an entire duplicated system of committees and procedures and will likely release some Friends to pursue other, less administrative, types of leadings.

Restructuring the regional meeting. Just as some monthly meetings become worship groups, some regional meetings might not be led to conduct any business. If Friends in the region feel strongly about gathering for worship or social reasons, and if these gatherings feel vital and Spirit-led, there is no reason I can see why a regional meeting could not continue to do this while simultaneously laying down all business functions and committees—with the possible exception of a task group nominated for the sole purpose of arranging the next gathering.

Of course, just as a worship group must be under the care of a monthly meeting (because worship groups do not own property or hold memberships), a region that does not conduct business might need to find a new group—such as a yearly meeting or another region—to steward its property and finances.

Reassessing our relationship with property and finances. When local meetings reassess their relationships with property, the question is generally whether the building is still supporting the ministries of the meeting or whether the meeting's energy is devoted mostly to supporting the building. For regional meetings that own property, answering this question might be more difficult, especially if the regional meeting owns and manages the property while it's primarily Friends in the local meetings who are using the property. The work of caring for the property is displaced by this arrangement, and it's very hard to tell whether the time, energy, and money spent maintaining it is appropriately balanced with the meeting's use of it.

Everything about the work of a regional meeting is less immediate than the work of a local meeting. Conversations and decisions take longer. Friends from one local meeting may not know Friends from another. And reflecting on the state of the regional meeting means reflecting on the institution of the region itself plus the condition of each of the local meetings within it. When the situation is that complex, and when we are engaging with questions about property and money (which tend to provoke heightened emotions), it can be very tempting to maintain the status quo—even if this means burning out a new set of trustees or property committee members every few years.

What would happen if the regional meeting reassessed its relationship with its property and its finances? What if Friends held a threshing session around the question, "Is our current investment of time and money in the physical properties we own still the way in which God would ask us to spend our resources?" Or, to take a step further back, "How does God ask us to use our resources at this time?"

Laying down the regional meeting. Some regional meetings, when they ask the question "do we still feel called to maintain the structure of a regional meeting?" will find that the answer is no. If that's the case, the most compelling reason to maintain a regional meeting structure is because the yearly meeting's book of discipline requires it. This does not seem to me like sufficient reason. After all, Friends dating back to the elders at Balby have recognized that advice from yearly meetings is a Light to walk by, not a set of absolute rules by which we must order our lives.

What would happen if regional meetings began to lay themselves down? Local meetings would either affiliate directly the yearly meeting or else join another region. In most cases in which regional meetings are struggling to function, the primary reason is that most Friends already either associate with their yearly meeting directly or don't associate with any group of Friends beyond their own local meetings. If this is true, then laying down the regional meetings would be an accurate reflection of the relationships that already exist.

Some regional meetings are serving essential functions. They may be thriving and beloved. When this is the case, Friends are very unlikely to feel led to lay down the region—and, as always, the meeting discerns its own future. Like any other Quaker institution, if the regional meeting as it currently exists is still supporting the community's ability to be faithful, then it should not be changed. But if we have the situation reversed and the regional meeting community is devoting its energy to keeping the region's institutional structures going, then we have a structural mismatch, and it's time to adapt the institution.

Transitions and Endings for Yearly Meetings

YEARLY MEETINGS ARE THE large associations of local meetings that historically met for business annually, although many now gather multiple times per year. Early Friends had only one yearly meeting, but when they began to evangelize across oceans, more became necessary.

These Friends never intended yearly meetings to become theologically or culturally distinct. They imagined that, through traveling ministers, Friends would continue to exchange revelations and insights across the entire Religious Society of Friends. But functionally, these new yearly meetings practiced corporate discernment separately, not as a whole Society, since Friends in distant countries could not be expected to travel to London every year by wooden sailing ship.

Anyone who thought through the matter carefully could have anticipated theological drift. Friends already knew from experience with individuals that we each hear from God imperfectly and that what we sense is often guided by culture and preconceptions and ego. Yearly meetings function no differently. Over time, the various yearly meetings drifted apart and sometimes formally disaffiliated from one another. New theological ideas or practices prompted some Friends to choose one way of being, others another. Even within yearly meetings, there were often splits, and some have later reunified.

Today, yearly meetings are markers of identity. Friends can and do make mostly-accurate assumptions about one another based on yearly meeting affiliation. We generally don't minute snide comments about "those others called Quakers," a commonly used phrase during the Hicksite-Orthodox split, but some of our feelings haven't evolved much.

The result of splits and disaffiliation is weakness. Due to schisms and the overall trend of dropping church attendance, most of our yearly meetings have decreased in membership by a startling percentage since the 1980s. To my knowledge, no yearly meetings in the United States are larger than they were fifty years ago. A few of our yearly meetings have sufficient funding and human resources (committee members or staff or both) to maintain their activities, but the majority are struggling. The institutional structure of the yearly meeting is no longer supporting the community of the whole yearly meeting. Friends who serve yearly meeting functions find themselves focused mostly on perpetuating yearly meeting functions. Friends who don't serve yearly meeting functions wonder why the yearly meeting exists at all.

Yearly meetings and other large Quaker organizations realize their structures are not working. Most have tried to address the problems multiple times. But the individual Friends who serve in yearly meeting positions have disproportionate influence over yearly meeting discernment (by virtue of being present when it happens), and nearly all of those Friends have some special interest in a particular yearly meeting activity. If they didn't, they wouldn't be serving on a yearly meeting committee.

The result is yearly meetings with bloated structures, each part of which originally had a specific purpose, each part of which is nearly impossible to lay down because some Friend is ready to fight for its existence. Yet, because our numbers have decreased so sharply, we cannot find enough Friends to serve in all the existing positions.

Some yearly meetings respond by hiring staff, and the yearly meetings that are very well-funded have, in some cases, developed very large staff structures, sometimes with a surprising proportion of employees who are not Friends. Other yearly meetings do not have sufficient funding to cover all of their activities and find themselves in a perpetual budget shortfall.

Our institutional structure is no longer supporting our community, and the situation will not improve unless we make significant changes. If we try to continue as we are, most of our yearly meetings will collapse. The only question is when this will happen and who or what will be harmed in the process.

So what are the options?

Before the Resurrection

Changing the committee structure. Most attempts to change a yearly meeting committee structure are akin to a game of musical chairs. Friends start with the premise that the committee structure must be simplified or downsized because not enough Friends are available to serve. But one Friend or another argues on behalf of continuing every committee. "The task of this group is too important to lose!" And that may well be the case. But Friends know there is a difference between a concern (a deep spiritual knowing that something is important) and a leading (a call from God to take specific action ourselves).

If not enough Friends are led to serve on a committee, the committee should be laid down. Most likely, if the committee has been understaffed, it hasn't been fulfilling its charge anyway, so let's be truthful about the state of our community. If the concern is sufficiently important, we can trust that God will lead someone to address it—just not, apparently, through service on this particular committee. Perhaps a Friend will take on the concern as a ministry. Or perhaps a group will rise up in a local or regional meeting.

Most of the work done by yearly meeting committees is work that early Friends would have expected ministers to do. These Friends, whose leadings were affirmed and supported by their local worshiping communities, did evangelism and religious education and publishing and witness. They traveled from one meeting to another, usually in pairs or with an elder, and they were accountable to the Friends they worked with and to their home communities. Sometime around the 1960s, Friends began shifting the work of ministers to the work of committees. It might have been an attempt to better organize the work, or it might have been a reaction to ministers outrunning their Guide. But committees are the most rigid approach to organizing work that is available to Friends—detailed charges, imposed calendars, predictable behavior patterns, formal nominations processes. This is the shift that has made yearly meeting structures so difficult to adapt.

Today, many ministers can work with distant Friends without ever leaving their computer screen. Affirming ministries is one pathway forward in a yearly meeting. If a Friend is stubbornly refusing to allow a committee to be laid down, it is possible that Friend is actually called to ministry but has never been told that is an available option.

Yearly meetings are also ideal settings for working groups and task groups. A working group is composed of Friends who have volunteered to work together on a particular concern, and a task group is composed of

Friends who are given a specific assignment and whose group is automatically laid down at its completion. Both of these structures are much more flexible than committees and are easier to raise up and to lay down.

Making staff transitions. Historically, Friends consider staff members to be released ministers—that is, members of our community with whom we anticipate working alongside. Released ministers receive financial support so that they can focus more time on their ministries.

In a yearly meeting setting, it can be difficult to remember that staff are actually released ministers. They seem disproportionately important because of the number of Friends they work with and their visibility, and at the same time, Friends throughout the yearly meeting feel entitled to make judgements about their work and criticize. We tend to want more observable results and often don't recognize the amount of invisible labor that is happening to keep the institution going.

If a yearly meeting is making staff transitions, it might begin by asking, "Do we need more staff, less staff, or different staff?"

If a yearly meeting can define specific types of work that need doing and that currently aren't being addressed, and if that yearly meeting has sufficient funding to add another staff position (at a rate of pay that is just), then that yearly meeting might release another minister to take on particular yearly meeting work.

If a yearly meeting has a consistent financial shortfall, and if staff is a primary expense, then that yearly meeting might reduce staff. Inevitably, Friends will ask the question, "How will we get the work done without our staff members?" It seems likely, if there is no reasonable way of getting the work done, that the yearly meeting is not actually called to do that work at this time. That may be a disconcerting thought, but as communities change, so does the work they are called to do.

And if a yearly meeting recognizes a structural mismatch, with one area of work being well-covered and another area being neglected, then that yearly meeting might need different staff. Perhaps, for example, a professional archivist or communications person used to be essential, but now there is a strong communications committee and no one helping meetings with religious education for children. The Friend who has been serving as an archivist is unlikely to have the right gifts or leadings to begin working in children's religious education instead, and so a change might need to be made.

Staff transitions might be even more difficult than changing committee structures. We know, when we make staff changes, that we are affecting someone's livelihood. At the same time, if a Friend's released ministry is no longer needed in the community, it's a significant problem for the whole community to continue devoting limited funding to it.

Moving to hybrid or online status. Many yearly meetings are experimenting with hybrid and online gatherings, and most are seeing shifts in participation as a result. New Friends are appearing online; a few familiar faces are staying away. When a meeting happens entirely or partly online, it is more accessible on average—that is, for most Friends, it is a net benefit rather than a net loss, even though the nature of online community is fundamentally different from in person community.

I've written in a prior section about online meetings becoming less geographically specific. For yearly meetings, this may be a blessing. Participation is just as easy for isolated Friends as for those who live in the yearly meeting's geographic or population center. And because online meetings are comparatively simple (no travel time, housing, or gasoline required), many yearly meetings are already gathering more often and doing more work.

The "doing more work" phenomenon is worth considering carefully. Are we led to do more work, or are we simply doing it because it is possible? To the extent that online gatherings add to yearly meeting staff or committee to-do lists, I'm not sure they are virtuous. But there is another way of approaching online conversations. Videoconferencing can be a platform for networking, an opportunity for Friends from one local meeting to connect with Friends from another local meeting, with no expertise needed on the part of the yearly meeting organizer. This more accurately reflects the original purpose of yearly meetings, which was to provide a network in which all Friends in the yearly meeting community could give and receive larger-than-local ministry. Suddenly, yearly meetings need not provide trainings from experts or one-on-one consultations. Instead, they can offer ways for Friends to help each other.

The non-geographic nature of online ministries also makes yearly meeting boundaries more porous than ever before. Trainings and projects that happen online can be open to Friends from other yearly meetings. In most cases, doing this is helpful to everyone. Friends from outside the yearly meeting receive access to opportunities that may not be available in their own yearly meetings. Friends within the yearly meeting receive connections with new people and new ideas, and a higher number of participants often makes the event livelier and more useful for everyone.

Transitions and Endings for Yearly Meetings

Merging with other yearly meetings. As Friends simplify committee structures, learn to affirm ministries, and develop online programs and events, I believe we are preparing to merge yearly meetings. It's unlikely we can reach approval to make the change all at once. Even if two or more yearly meetings are each struggling for lack of participation or resources, there is a certain resistance to merging that arises from the ideological identity pieces of yearly meeting affiliation.

But if we begin with shared projects and an exchange of ministries, we can build interpersonal relationships and begin to understand how much we have in common. Over time, we may become ready to discuss an institutional merger. Combining two or more yearly meetings would require answering a lot of questions: which ministries and committees will continue, and which will be laid down? Will we blend our staff structures (if we have them)? Who will control endowments or property? Whose traditions will influence our minuting procedures, our report deadlines, our annual gathering talent shows? These are all cultural questions, though, and if we have agreement on the underlying spiritual principles, we can sort through procedures.

Restructuring the yearly meeting. Could there ever be such a thing as one yearly meeting under the care of another? Perhaps a yearly meeting could restructure as a region and then become part of another yearly meeting. In this situation, the yearly meeting need not lose its identity entirely, but it would have a wider group of Friends with whom to build relationships and share work and resources.

It's worth noting that in the twenty-first century, two yearly meetings that enter a new type of relationship would not necessarily need to be geographically adjoined. If yearly meeting business were held in hybrid fashion, with the in-person portion rotating between geographic areas, there could be a successful covenant relationship across significant distances.

Laying down the yearly meeting. What would happen if a yearly meeting laid itself down? I can't see any reason why a yearly meeting, like a local meeting, might not have a natural life cycle. Here's a reminder of the questions we can ask when wondering if it's time for a meeting to be laid down:

Is the meeting no longer capable of taking on *essential functions*? (The essential functions of a yearly meeting might be gathering annually, conducting business, fulfilling its financial obligations, and supporting its monthly meetings reliably, plus providing support and accountability for its at-large members if it has any.)

Before the Resurrection

Do Friends focus on *survival rather than ministry* when discussing the future? (For a yearly meeting, this might mean that more time is spent talking about institutional struggles than engaging with impactful projects or prophetic messages.)

Is the *average attendance at yearly meeting gatherings shrinking*?

Are all or nearly all of us *past retirement age*?

Do Friends struggle to provide *mutual care* and *interact lovingly* because of feelings of scarcity, anxiety, or irreconcilable priorities?

Does the meeting focus most of its time *on internal functions*, such as committee reports and procedural matters, rather than ministry beyond the group gathered?

Do many Friends in the yearly meeting *feel disconnected from the yearly meeting*, as if the yearly meeting is some distant institution rather than a large covenant community of Friends?

Is the yearly meeting not *vital*—not experiencing the presence of God in worship—or not *viable*—not having enough financial or human resources to keep going?

I think there are yearly meetings that are nearing the ends of their life cycles. But what does it look like for a yearly meeting to lay itself down? How would that happen?

Like a local or regional meeting, a yearly meeting is not automatically laid down when it has reached the final stage of the life cycle. Because it has a legal and procedural existence, it will continue until we actively and deliberately lay it down, even if it were to collapse someday and become a ghost meeting. The *covenant community* of Friends that composes a yearly meeting will not vanish without warning; we will continue to exist as long as we are alive and worshiping. But an institutional structure certainly *could* collapse for lack of participation if we allow outsized structures to continue unaddressed and unmodified. If an institutional collapse were to happen, there would be considerable difficulty figuring out who would disperse the yearly meeting's assets and help monthly meetings find new associations. Most likely, a small group of trustees would wind up making decisions for all of the Friends in the yearly meeting.

Our yearly meetings are even less likely than our local meetings to be saved by a miracle. A local meeting might suddenly expand by four families moving into town all in the same year, doubling or tripling the participation in the meeting, but for a yearly meeting to experience the same thing, four new families would have to appear in every local meeting. The odds are slim.

As I've already said, there are many ways in which a yearly meeting can respond to changing circumstances. We can adapt committee structures, hire staff, merge yearly meetings, restructure into regional meetings. . .but if none of these things feel right or sufficient, then we might consider laying down the yearly meeting.

Like a local meeting, a yearly meeting could consider its legacy. What has historically been important to this yearly meeting? How would we hope to be resurrected, remembering that resurrection is not the same as resuscitation? Perhaps our ancestors played a role in women's suffrage, and since then, we have been advocating for gender equality. If that's the case, undesignated yearly meeting resources might go toward education for girls. Or maybe our yearly meeting had many members of the Underground Railroad and has been working on anti-racism concerns in the 21st century. If that's who God has called us to be, our undesignated yearly meeting resources might be given to an historically black church. Or it could be that our yearly meeting has overseas missions and always has. If that's the case, our undesignated funds might all go into an endowment to support them.

But *how* could Friends lay down a yearly meeting—or merge two yearly meetings, or restructure into a region? How could we do this when we don't have a modern-day model for it? Let's look at some steps:

Say it out loud. Someone has to say, "We might be called to lay down the yearly meeting or merge with another yearly meeting." The reactions are likely to vary enormously. Some Friends will be horrified, others alarmed, others certain it's impossible. Some Friends will be apathetic, some delighted, some angry that anyone would say such a thing.

Commit to Spirit-led discernment. This might actually be quite hard. Friends may not be able to agree whether the yearly meeting should even consider such significant steps. The first matter for discernment might be whether to enter a period of discernment. This can begin at a yearly meeting gathering or in a group composed of representatives, but it must include Friends in local meetings. Entering discernment about steps this radical would probably require Friends who were willing to travel, in person, to local meetings and explain the situation and available possibilities.

Worship. Friends throughout the yearly meeting might enter a period of worship and prayer, both within their local meetings and online with the rest of the yearly meeting. What is God's will for this yearly meeting now?

Talk about it. Friends will have a lot of questions, and they will want to express a lot of concerns. What will happen to this ministry, or that meeting, or these staff members? As much as possible, it helps to have such conversations in real time. Sending minutes back and forth often creates bad feelings, since long delays can make it feel as though contributions aren't being taken seriously, and a lot can be communicated (and softened) in real-time conversations through body language and tone.

Make sure everyone knows what's being considered. If one of the difficulties in a yearly meeting is a feeling of disconnection from local meetings, this is an especially crucial step. Sending a mass email might not be sufficient. Friends might not take such a communication seriously or might not believe their input is genuinely wanted. Friends will need lots of time to ask questions, work through emotional reactions, and enter genuine discernment together.

Involve the wider world of Friends. The Quaker rumor mill is strong. It is not possible that a yearly meeting would keep significant discernment a secret. If the yearly meeting is considering restructuring or merging or laying itself down, Friends in other yearly meetings will know about this, and if they are not given accurate information about what's happening, they will very likely make up stories—not maliciously, but because this is human nature. But the wider world of Friends can actually help. They can hold the yearly meeting's discernment in prayer. They can engage in intervisitation. They might even provide temporary financial support, if that's needed to keep things going until the discernment process can be completed. No yearly meeting need navigate this kind of situation alone.

Hold threshing sessions. A threshing session is a period of open worship in which Friends are invited to express their feelings, their thoughts, and their leadings regarding a potential change. Threshing sessions are different from business meetings because no decision is anticipated. They are purely for the purpose of listening and being listened to, and they can help prepare us for business meetings in which we do intend to make decisions.

Find sense of the meeting. Eventually, probably after several years, it will be time to find sense of the meeting—or, in the case of a merger, sense of the meetings. This will probably happen at a yearly meeting gathering (in person or online), but only after a lengthy period of time for Friends throughout the yearly meeting to know what is happening and contribute to the discernment process, so that no one is rushed into the decision or left out because they're not able to attend a gathering on one specific day.

Transitions and Endings for Yearly Meetings

Care for one another during the transition. What will happen to each local meeting? What will happen to each yearly meeting ministry? There will need to be a plan in place before the action is finalized. Friends will also need help working through the transition, whatever it is, spiritually and emotionally. It will not be possible for one small group of Friends to provide pastoral care to everyone who might need it throughout the yearly meeting, but Friends can be empowered—even trained—to reach out to one another. Encouraging intervisitation might also be helpful, so that no local meeting feels isolated during the transition.

Work through the practical and legal tasks. If two yearly meetings are merging, or if one yearly meeting is restructuring into a region or laying itself down, the legal and logistical implications will be enormous. Someone will have to sort through what happens to the yearly meeting's property, investment funds, endowments, staff members, and ministries. And depending on what type of transition is happening, local meetings and regional meetings might simultaneously need to do the same. Because these practicalities might take a long time, Friends should consider how best to keep everyone up to date. Can there be a page on a website that's updated weekly? Can there be videoconference calls in which questions are answered?

Mark the transition with an event. When the transition is complete—whatever it is—Friends can gather to celebrate, to grieve, or (probably) to do both. This gathering should center worship but not be limited only to worship; sharing food and having conversations will also be important for the community.

Any institutional transition is uniquely difficult for a yearly meeting. The size and geographic range of the community presents practical obstacles for the corporate discernment essential to the practice of Quakerism. We say the meeting discerns its own future, but how can the meeting do this? The whole of the yearly meeting will not be in one place at one time. And if each meeting is given formal representatives, those representatives often feel beholden to the positions of their meetings, which makes corporate discernment impossible because the process of discernment is about listening and becoming spiritually convinced—which means we must be able to change our positions. So many yearly meetings default to conducting discernment with whatever Friends come to the discernment gathering. But this, too, is difficult, because any Friend who is unable to appear at the chosen time and place is by default left out, and those Friends who choose to come are often the ones with especially strong feelings and may not find a sense of the meeting that accurately reflects the sense of the yearly meeting as a whole.

The only way forward that I can see is to allow the discernment to take place in many smaller groups over a long period of time. Local meetings, regional meetings, and other groups could hold threshing sessions in a variety of locations and online. We should avoid, whenever possible, asking these smaller groups to submit the results of their discernment in writing because then we are left with a collection of minutes, and minutes do not listen to one another when gathered and do not progress under the leadings of Spirit. Instead, the best way forward that I can see is to ask as many Friends as can to attend multiple threshing sessions over time, so that they are able to speak and listen in groups of various compositions. In time, a genuine sense of the yearly meeting may begin to emerge, and it can then be affirmed at a yearly meeting gathering, even if not everyone is able to attend that final meeting for business.

What Resurrection Might Look Like

Quakers are a resurrection people, beginning with the story of Jesus. We demonstrate our faith in resurrection every time we enter corporate discernment, fully expecting the inbreaking of Light. Redemption is always possible, even when our circumstances have pushed us to the brink of despair.

But resurrection is not the same as resuscitation. Early Friends emphasized spiritual transformation, not spiritual restoration. When have we ever said that God's will is to maintain the status quo?

Those statements are how I started this book. It feels obvious to me that some things are ending. An historical form of Quakerism, composed of local and regional and yearly meetings, is winding down in North America and western Europe. We can fight to preserve it unchanged until the moment it dies—or we can recognize that God is doing a new thing, and we can adapt to our new reality. By simplifying, merging, and laying down meetings, we are releasing spiritual energy and resources so that God may use them in new and exciting ways.

If resurrection is not resuscitation, what will resurrection look like? I can't claim to know for sure, but I can name some new life that I already see rising.

The Friends Church in East Africa. Quakerism is growing in several parts of the world, but nowhere faster than in East Africa. There are theological and cultural differences between the Quakerism in East Africa and the Quakerism familiar to most readers of this book, but there are also commonalities. Friends in East Africa affirm the equality of men and women in places where this is profoundly counter-cultural. They support women who are called into ministry. Friends in East Africa have peace ministries, often extremely responsive and vital ones, developing skills for nonviolent cooperation among groups with historical rivalry. They are opening and running preschools and primary schools and working in communities to reduce early marriage (particularly of girls under age eighteen) and eliminate the practice of female genital mutilation. Friends in East Africa run hospitals and dispensaries and emergency feeding programs and clean water ministries. And they affirm that "Christ has come to teach his people himself."

Spontaneous and non-traditional worship groups. Historically, Friends have said that worship groups begin when a monthly meeting plants them. But that's not happening much anymore. Instead, worship groups are springing up in cities and small towns and sometimes online among Friends or who may or may not have any formal affiliation to another meeting. Some of these worship groups later request membership in a yearly meeting. Others do not and are never formally, externally recognized.

Spiritual formation courses. I can think, just offhand, of at least six multi-year Quaker spiritual formation courses that have been offered to individuals since 2015, plus another three offered to whole meetings. Through courses like these, Friends experience a different pathway to spiritual community and transformation, not through a regional or yearly meeting program but through ministries supported through non-traditional institutional channels.

Alternative membership pathways. I've lost track of the number of yearly meetings that now offer direct individual membership to the yearly meeting, and umbrella organizations are starting to offer direct membership to local meetings unaffiliated with any yearly meeting. There's no uniformity in how these channels work or precisely why they're being offered, but they are evidence of new configurations of covenant communities.

Retreat centers. Quaker retreat centers have existed for a long time—at least several generations—but historically, Friends visited them and then returned to their local meeting communities. Now, retreat centers are primary connections to Quakerism for many Friends. In addition to in-person workshops and other educational programming, several retreat centers offer worship and other opportunities online, so there are even Friends who would identify a retreat center as their primary spiritual home despite having never physically been there.

Young adult and youth groups. There are many strong communities of young adults and teens, some small, some large, and many not connected to any particular local meeting. Friends who are part of these groups often identify the group as a primary spiritual home. At a certain point, this presents a problem—what happens when a Friend ages out?—but it's nevertheless a genuine phenomenon. For some, the young adult or youth group is the sole experience of Quaker community.

Spiritual accountability and faithfulness groups. These groups are known by a number of names and are structured in various ways, but they are small groups of Friends who meet together regularly for worship and discussion of their spiritual lives. The conversation is deep, and Friends encourage one another in faithfulness. Some Friends in such groups are also affiliated with more traditional worship communities, while others are not.

Quaker schools. Most Quaker schools in North America and western Europe are no longer under the care of meetings and are either entirely separated from or just loosely connected to formal Quakerism. But some of the students who graduate from Quaker schools do identify as Quakers. No one tracks these graduates, so there is no available data about whether and how they continue a Quaker practice throughout their lifetimes.

Witness groups. A few fair-sized groups now exist that are primarily organized around Quaker witness, including demonstrations and civil disobedience. They are deeply grounded in worship but center on social change as their purpose, and they are some Friends' primary or only Quaker community.

Intentional communities. These are groups of people, some Friends, some not Friends, who live in close relationship and use Quaker principles and practices to guide their relationships. Some include whole families, others only adults; some exist in single buildings, others in neighborhoods. But worship, discernment, and Quaker testimonies are central to these communities.

There are other manifestations of Quaker community that I haven't seen but can imagine.

Service and advocacy collectives might be organized communities of Friends and non-Friends who exist for the purpose of mutual service and improving a neighborhood community. Such groups could use Quaker worship and discernment to nurture the spiritual gifts of their members, develop safer and healthier neighborhoods in which to live, and work with governments and civil services agencies.

Other Friends could crystalize around *coffee shop or restaurant ministries,* as have sprung up in some other faith communities. In such groups, it's not that the meeting has a restaurant but that the meeting *is* a restaurant, a place where people come for nutritional, tasty, well-priced food. Those who need it can receive a meal for free, and friendly conversation and hospitality are assumed as part of the experience. Such a ministry might employ those who are struggling to find jobs and might initiate or support community gardens as sources of fruits and vegetables.

Quaker community might thrive in *mutual aid societies*, in which individuals pool their money so that one member can attend school or start a business or receive emergency health care, with the assumption that the receiver will continue to contribute to the group financially well into the future after receiving assistance. Imagine a mutual aid society that includes a financial relationship and a spiritual relationship, based in worship and affirming Divine leadings.

Quakerism, as a theology, can thrive anywhere among any group of people that listens to God together, discerns corporately, and supports each member in faithfulness. I hope and believe that new manifestations will draw from the rich bodies of wisdom and the generations of revelations that came before, including what has been received from our ancestors already and what we living Friends will leave behind.

Just imagine what might happen if we are open to the signs of resurrection among us and ready to embrace God's new things. . .if we can borrow from the passionately experimental nature of early Friends and, by repurposing our budgets as financial support for ministry or donating endowments and buildings from laid-down meetings, invest in forms that are unproven but alive with the presence of Christ.

Will we Friends squirrel away our financial resources, our time, and our energy? Will we invest them in propping up the old ways, hoping for resuscitation?

Or will we honor God's unfolding story by right-sizing our institutional structures and releasing the excess for what Isaiah calls "a new thing"?

A Conversation Guide for Friends Using Readings from the Bible

IN THIS SECTION, YOU will find a conversation guide drawing from Biblical texts that will help you reflect on the state of your meeting and some of the principles discussed in this book. You will need more than one gathering to work through the readings and the discussion questions. There is no reason why you must use all of the readings or use them in this order. Feel free to adapt the suggestions for your own use.

This conversation guide is not intended to bring you to any decision about the next steps for your meeting. Instead, it will help you reflect on your meeting's history and present condition through Scripture, and it may provide a new perspective on the possibility of change.

Take the readings one at a time. Read the verse or verses. Spend some time discussing the first set of questions (directly related to the Scripture) and then the second set of questions (more directly related to your meeting).

> "Now the Lord God had planted a garden in the east, in Eden; and there he put the man he had formed...the Lord God took the man and put him in the Garden of Eden to work it and take care of it." (Genesis 2:8 & 2:15)

What was Adam's relationship to the Garden of Eden? Although the Garden had been planted by God, Adam was asked to tend it. In what way did tending the garden benefit Adam? What might his responsibilities have been?

Whose responsibility is it to tend your meeting? In what way does tending the meeting benefit those who do it? What are their responsibilities?

Before the Resurrection

> ". . . the land is mine and you reside in my land as foreigners and strangers." (Leviticus 25:23b)

In Leviticus 25, God provides instructions to the Israelites regarding how they are to use the land they've been given. The instructions are complex and lengthy, but God reminds the Israelites that the land belongs to Him and that they are only residing on it. Why would God remind the Israelites of this?

Does your meeting also belong to God? If that is true, what are the implications for your community?

> "The temple I am going to build will be great, because our God is greater than all other gods." (2 Chronicles 2:5)

When Solomon built the temple, he chose talented craftsmen and purchased the highest quality materials because he believed that creating an expensive, beautiful temple would be the best way to honor God. What do you believe is the best way to honor God?

How does your meeting honor God?

> "The daughters of Zelophehad son of Hepher, the son of Gilead, the son of Makir, the son of Manasseh, belonged to the clans of Manasseh son of Joseph. The names of the daughters were Mahlah, Noah, Hoglah, Milkah and Tirzah. They came forward and stood before Moses, Eleazar the priest, the leaders and the whole assembly at the entrance to the tent of meeting and said, 'Our father died in the wilderness. He was not among Korah's followers, who banned together against the Lord, but he died for his own sin and left no sons. Why should our father's name disappear from his clan because he had no son? Give us property among our father's relatives.' So Moses brought their case before the Lord, and the Lord said to him, 'What Zelophehad's daughters are saying is right. You must certainly give them property as an inheritance among their father's relatives and give their father's inheritance to them.'" (Numbers 27:1–7)

The law in Moses' time said that only men could inherit property, but Zelophehad's daughters believed this was wrong. When they asked that Moses reconsider and Moses prayed to God, God affirmed that the daughters were right. They should inherit. What does this tell us about the nature of God?

A Conversation Guide for Friends Using Readings from the Bible

What inheritance have Friends in your meeting received? What inheritance might you ask God to grant you? Are you prepared to accept a surprising response from God, should you receive one?

> "Therefore everyone who hears these words of mine and puts them into practice is like a wise man who built his house on the rock. The rains came down, the streams rose, and the winds blew and beat against that house; yet it did not fall, because it had its foundation on the rock." (Matthew 7:24–25)

In this famous parable, Jesus is comparing those who hear and practice his words to those who do not. In a literal sense, how does it feel to be in a secure house during a storm? Has hearing and practicing the words of Jesus made you feel similarly?

What does it mean for a Quaker meeting to be built on a foundation of rock, as Jesus talks about in these verses?

> "The Lord had said to Abram, 'Go from your country, your people and your father's household to the land I will show you. I will make you into a great nation, and I will bless you; I will make your name great, and you will be a blessing.'" (Genesis 12:1–2)

In this text, God is commanding Abram to leave behind all that is familiar and trust that the new destination will be a good place. Have you ever had such an experience? What was it like?

What might your meeting be called to leave behind in order to follow God's next leadings for you?

> "When you reap the harvest of your land, do not reap to the very edges of your field or gather the gleanings of your harvest. Leave them for the poor and for the foreigner residing among you. I am the Lord your God." (Leviticus 23:22)

Here, God commands the Israelites to leave behind some of what their land grows. Why would God give these instructions? How do you think the Israelites might have felt about this?

In what ways does your meeting share its resources with people who are not part of it? Can you think of other ways your meeting might be called to share its resources? How does this feel?

> "Suppose one of you wants to build a tower. Won't you first sit down and estimate the cost to see if you have enough money to complete it? For if you lay the foundation and are not able to finish

it, everyone who sees it will ridicule you, saying, 'This person began to build and wasn't able to finish.'" (Luke 14:28–30)

Jesus shares this brief parable as part of a series of parables about being a disciple. What might he have been trying to say?

Has your meeting ever tried to do something and discovered it did not have the necessary resources to do it successfully? How did that feel?

> "For six years you are to sow your fields and harvest the crops, but during the seventh year let the land lie unplowed and unused. Then the poor among your people may get food from it, and the wild animals may eat what is left. Do the same with your vineyard and your olive grove." (Exodus 23:10–11)

Why might God have asked the Israelites to let their land lie fallow every seven years?

What is the role of rest in your Quaker meeting?

> "For we know that if the earthly tent we live in is destroyed, we have a building from God, an eternal house in heaven, not built by human hands." (2 Corinthians 5:1)

This passage is a metaphorical reference to the human body but reminds us that all things die. When you have lost someone or something dear to you, how have you found comfort? From where does your hope come?

When something difficult has happened to your meeting, how have you found comfort together? From where does your hope come?

> "By faith Abraham, when called to go to a place he would later receive as his inheritance, obeyed and went, even though he did not know where he was going. By faith he made his home in the promised land like a stranger in a foreign country; he lived in tents, as did Isaac and Jacob, who were heirs with him of the same promise. For he was looking forward to the city with foundations, whose architect and builder is God." (Hebrews 11:8–10)

In this Scripture, we are reminded of Abraham's journey of faith. Who in your life has been an example of faithfulness to you?

What transitions do you foresee your meeting may be called to make in order to be faithful?

> "By the rivers of Babylon we sat and wept when we remembered Zion. There on the poplars we hung our harps, for there our captors

asked us for songs, our tormentors demanded songs of joy; they said, 'Sing us one of the songs of Zion!' How can we sing the songs of the Lord while in a foreign land? If I forget you, Jerusalem, may my right hand forget its skill. May my tongue cling to the roof of my mouth if I do not remember you, if I do not consider Jerusalem my highest joy." (Psalm 137:1–6)

The people are remembering Zion while in captivity in Babylon. What about the passage feels familiar to you? Have you ever had an experience like this?

Suppose that your meeting were called to lay itself down or to change in some significant way. Would it still be possible to sing the songs of the Lord? Why or why not? How would it feel?

"Then they set out, and the terror of God fell on the towns all around them so that no one pursued them. Jacob and all the people with him came to Luz (that is, Bethel) in the land of Canaan. There he built an altar, and he called the place El Bethel, because it was there that God revealed himself to him when he was fleeing from his brother." (Genesis 35:5–7)

Old Testament prophets often build altars to remember important events, usually powerful encounters with God, that had occurred in a particular place. When you have a transformative or important experience, is there anything you do to help yourself remember it?

What are some of the things God has done in your meeting that you would never want to forget?

A Conversation Guide for Friends Using Readings from Early Quakerism

IN THIS SECTION, YOU will find a conversation guide drawing from early Friends' writings that will help you reflect the state of your meeting and some of the principles discussed in this book. You will need more than one gathering to work through the readings and the discussion questions. There is no reason why you must use all of the readings or use them in this order. Feel free to adapt the suggestions for your own use.

This conversation guide will not bring you to a particular decision about the next steps for your meeting. Instead, it will help you reflect on your meeting's history and present condition, and it may provide a new perspective on the possibility of change.

Read the quotations together one at a time. Then, take a few minutes to reflect on the query either in open discussion or in worship sharing format, as the group prefers.

> "If you do any thing in your own wills, then you tempt God; but stand still in that power that brings peace."[1]

What do you think Fox meant by this? When you enter a discernment process with a group, what do you do with your "own will"?

> "We see that the teachings of the divine spirit have been the same in all ages. It has led to truth, to goodness, to justice, to love."[2]

What have you learned about "the divine spirit" from the history of your meeting or from the Friends who came before you?

1. Fox, "Tenth Epistle."
2. Mott, "Sermon at Yardleyville."

A Conversation Guide for Friends Using Readings from Early Quakerism

> "No clear impressions, either from above or from without, can be received by a mind turbid with excitement and agitated by a crowd of distractions. The stillness needed for the clear shining of light within is incompatible with hurry."[3]

Are you able to find a place of stillness as you consider the future of your meeting? Is anything making this difficult? Would anything help?

> "Whatever a man trusts in, that he makes his God, whether it is gold or silver, or the honors and pleasures of this world; if he trusts in these things, he makes them his God."[4]

In what do you trust?

> "Lord, grant a little help, quiet and enlighten my heart, that I may see what to do, and what to leave undone."[5]

Have you had the experience as a meeting of trying to do more than you've been able to do? What has this felt like? How do Elizabeth Fry's words speak to you (or not) in this situation?

> "The love of money is apt to increase almost imperceptibly. That which was at first laboured after under the pressure of necessary duty may, without great watchfulness, steal upon the affections, and gradually withdraw the heart of God. The danger depends not upon how much a man has, but upon how much his heart is set upon what he has, and upon accumulating more."[6]

How do you feel personally about the property or financial assets of your meeting? Have you ever had the experience of the love of money stealing upon your affections? What is your own sense of right relationship with money?

> "To turn all the treasures we possess into the channel of universal love becomes the business of our lives."[7]

If your meeting were to turn all its treasures into "the channel of universal love," what might it do? There is, of course, more than one answer. What might one way look like?

3. Stephen, "Light Arising: Thoughts on the Central Radiance."
4. Crisp, "The Divine Monitor: or, Light From Heaven."
5. Fry, *Memoir of the Life of Elizabeth Fry, with Extracts from Her Journal and Letters*.
6. Yearly Meeting in London 1858.
7. Woolman, "A Plea for the Poor."

Before the Resurrection

> "This is to me the hour of greatest joy I ever had in this world. No ear can hear, no tongue can utter, and no heart can understand the sweet incomes and the refreshings of the spirit of the Lord, which I now feel."[8]

Mary Dyer spoke these words in the moments before her death by execution. What might she have meant? What might we learn from Mary Dyer?

> "Abundantly sufficient for our help is the grace afforded us! Let all but keep to it, and then safe are their steppings, and sure their preservation; for, however severe their trials, the Lord will be near them."[9]

Do these words feel true? How has your meeting received help or grace?

> "Our life is love, and peace, and tenderness; and bearing one with another, and forgiving one another, and not laying accusations one against another; but praying one for another, and helping one another up with a tender hand."[10]

How have you experienced this type of life in your meeting? Does your meeting extend these ideas beyond your meeting space into your neighborhood or into the world? How do you, or how could you?

> "Truth will not lose ground by being tried."[11]

Are you comfortable with trying experiments as you try to find the right way forward for your meeting?

> "The true faith changeth not, which is the gift of God, and a mystery held in a pure conscience. Our faith, our church, our unity in the Spirit, and our Word, at which we tremble, was in the beginning before your church-made faiths, and our unity, church and fellowship will stand when they are all ended."[12]

If your meeting changes—or even ends—what will *not* be lost?

---

8. Dyer, her last words before execution.
9. Scott, *The Journal of Job Scott.*
10. Penington, "To Friends in Amersham."
11. Penington, letter to Elizabeth Stonar.
12. Fox, *The Journal of George Fox.*

Bibliography

Bridges, William, with Susan Bridges. *Transitions: Making Sense of Life's Changes.* New York: Hachette Books, 2019.
Cafferata, Gail. *The Last Pastor: Faithfully Steering a Closing Church.* Louisville, KY: Westminster John Knox Press, 2020.
Crisp, Stephen. "The Divine Monitor; or, Light From Heaven." https://artflsrv04.uchicago.edu/philologic4.7/EVANS/navigate/3331/7.
Elliott, Dirk. *Vital Merger: A New Church Start Approach that Joins Church Families Together.* United States of America: Fun & Done, 2013.
Fox, George. *The Journal of George Fox.* London: Thomas Northcott, 1694.
Frank, Thomas Edward. *The Soul of the Congregation: An Invitation to Congregational Reflection.* Nashville: Abingdon, 2000.
Friends World Committee for Consultation Section of the Americas. "FWCC Census of Friends Shows Declines, But More Research Is Needed." https://fwccamericas.org/_wp/2022/09/07/fwcc-census-of-friends-shows-declines-but-more-research-is-needed.
Fry, Elizabeth. *Memoir of the Life of Elizabeth Fry, with Extracts from Her Journal and Letters.* Great Britain: Charles Gilpin, 1847.
Gaede, Beth Ann, ed. *Ending with Hope: A Resource for Closing Congregations.* Lanham, MD: Rowman & Littlefield, 2002.
Gray, Stephen, and Franklin Dumond. *Legacy Churches.* St. Charles, IL: ChurchSmart Resources, 2009.
Hilliard, Linda M., and Gretchen J. Switzer. *Finishing With Grace: A Guide to Selling, Merging, and Closing Your Church.* United States of America: Booklocker.com Inc., 2010.
Irwin, L. Gail. *Toward the Better Country: Church Closure and Resurrection.* Eugene, OR: Resource Publications, 2014.
Mott, Lucretia. "A Sermon Delivered at Yardleyville." *The Liberator*, 1858.
Moulton, Phillip P., ed. *The Journal and Major Essays of John Woolman.* New York: Oxford University Press, 1971.
Penington, Isaac. "Letter to Elizabeth Stonar." York: James Hunton, 1828.
———. "To Friends in Amersham." York: James Hunton, 1828.

Bibliography

Rogers, Horatio. *Mary Dyer of Rhode Island, the Quaker Martyr That Was Hanged on Boston Common, June 1, 1660*. Providence, RI: Preston and Rounds, 1896.

Scott, Job. *The Journal of Job Scott*. New York: Isaac Collins, 1797.

Stephen, Caroline. *Light Arising; Thoughts on the Central Radiance*. Philadelphia: John C. Winston, 1908.

Woolf, Michael. "Denominations Are Dying. But the Church Can Still Thrive." https://sojo.net/biography/michael-woolf.

Yearly Meeting in London 1858. https://qfp.quaker.org.uk/passage/20-58/.

www.ingramcontent.com/pod-product-compliance
Lightning Source LLC
Chambersburg PA
CBHW071213160426
43196CB00011B/2278